THE LITTLE BLACK FISH

ORIGINAL STORY WRITTEN BY SAMAD BEHRANGI
ART AND DESIGN BY BIZHAN KHODABANDEH
PUBLISHED BY ROSARIUM PUBLISHING

THE LITTLE BLACK FISH

ORIGINAL STORY WRITTEN BY SAMAD BEHRANGI
ART AND DESIGN BY BIZHAN KHODABANDEH
PUBLISHED BY ROSARIUM PUBLISHING

FIRST EDITION

COMIC ADAPTATION, COVER ILLUSTRATION
COPYRIGHT 2015 BIZHAN KHODABANDEH

TRANSLATION COPYRIGHT 2015
BY BIZHAN KHODABANDEH

PRINTED IN CANADA

ROSARIUM **R**

ROSARIUMPUBLISHING.COM
PO BOX 544, GREENBELT, MD 20768-0544

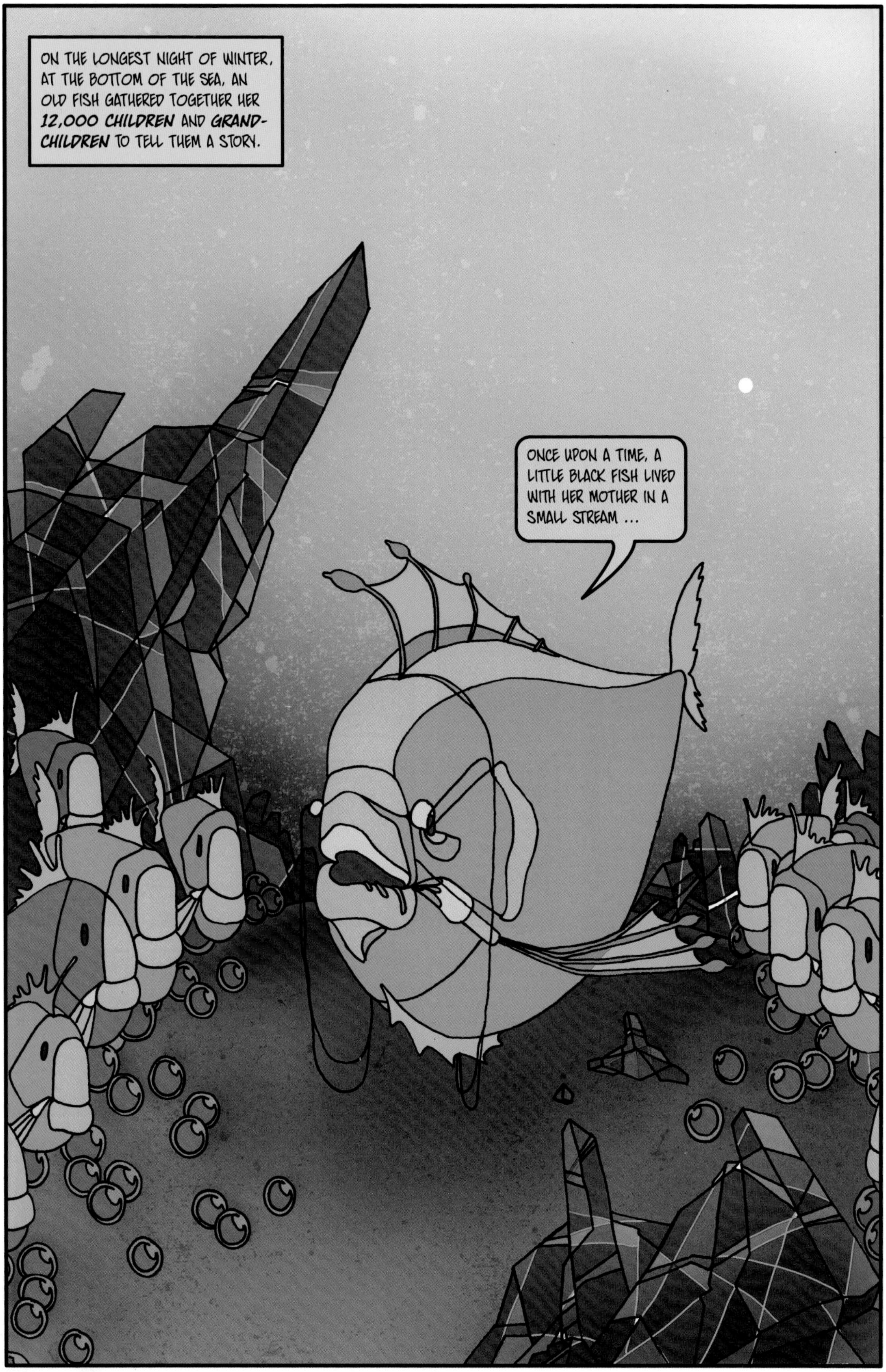
ON THE LONGEST NIGHT OF WINTER, AT THE BOTTOM OF THE SEA, AN OLD FISH GATHERED TOGETHER HER **12,000 CHILDREN** AND **GRAND-CHILDREN** TO TELL THEM A STORY.
ONCE UPON A TIME, A LITTLE BLACK FISH LIVED WITH HER MOTHER IN A SMALL STREAM ...

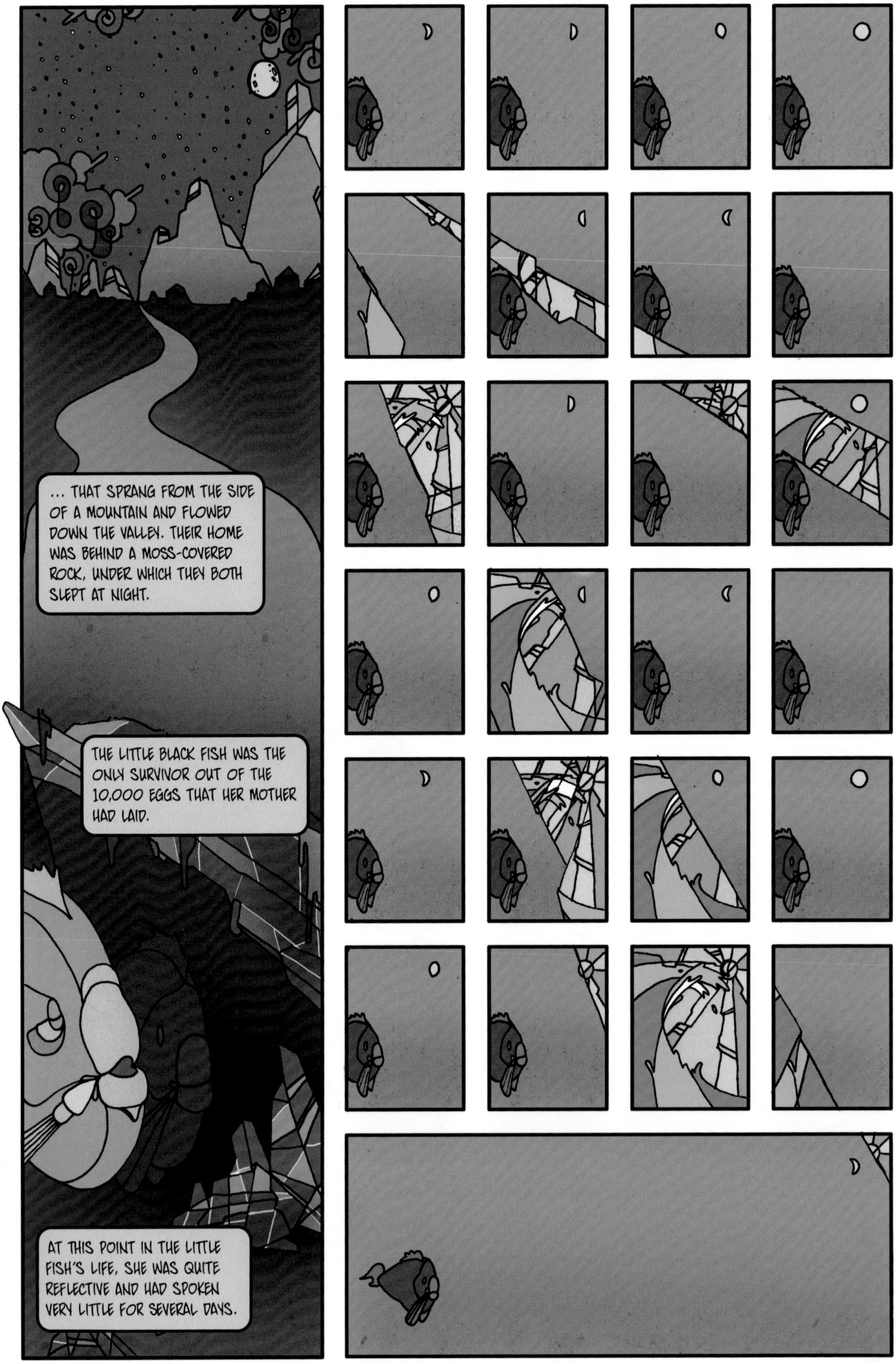
... THAT SPRANG FROM THE SIDE OF A MOUNTAIN AND FLOWED DOWN THE VALLEY. THEIR HOME WAS BEHIND A MOSS-COVERED ROCK, UNDER WHICH THEY BOTH SLEPT AT NIGHT.
THE LITTLE BLACK FISH WAS THE ONLY SURVIVOR OUT OF THE 10,000 EGGS THAT HER MOTHER HAD LAID.
AT THIS POINT IN THE LITTLE FISH'S LIFE, SHE WAS QUITE REFLECTIVE AND HAD SPOKEN VERY LITTLE FOR SEVERAL DAYS.

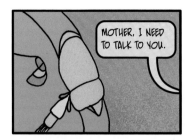

MOTHER, I NEED TO TALK TO YOU.

COME, ON CHILD. THIS ISN'T A GOOD TIME TO TALK.

SAVE YOUR WORDS FOR WHEN WE GO SWIMMING AROUND.

NO, MOTHER!

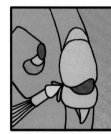

I CAN'T SWIM IN CIRCLES ANY LONGER. I **MUST** LEAVE THIS PLACE.

ARE YOU SERIOUS? DO YOU **REALLY** WANT TO LEAVE?

YES, MOTHER, I MUST GO. I NEED TO LEAVE AND SEE WHERE THE STREAM ENDS. I HAVE BEEN WONDERING WHERE IT ENDS ... AND I HAVEN'T BEEN ABLE TO THINK ABOUT ANYTHING ELSE. I STAY AWAKE THINKING ABOUT IT. I HAVE DECIDED TO GO AND FIND OUT FOR MYSELF. I WANT TO KNOW WHAT IS HAPPENING IN OTHER PLACES.

WHEN I WAS A CHILD, I USED TO THINK A LOT LIKE THAT. BUT, MY DEAR, A STREAM HAS NO BEGINNING AND NO END. THAT'S THE WAY IT IS. THE STREAM JUST FLOWS AND NEVER GOES ANYWHERE.

BUT, MOTHER DEAR, ISN'T IT TRUE THAT EVERYTHING COMES TO AN END? NIGHTS END, DAYS END, SO DO WEEKS, MONTHS, YEARS ...

PUT ASIDE THESE THOUGHTS. LET US GO FOR A SWIM. NOW IS THE TIME TO **SWIM**, NOT TO **TALK**.

NO, MOTHER! I'M TIRED OF THIS AIMLESS SWIMMING, I WANT TO MOVE ON AND SEE WHAT'S HAPPENING ELSE-WHERE. DO NOT THINK THAT SOMEONE HAS PUT ME UP TO THIS, BECAUSE, BELIEVE ME, I'VE HAD THESE THOUGHTS FOR A LONG TIME. YET STILL, I'VE LEARNED MANY THINGS FROM OTHERS. I LEARNED THAT WHEN MOST FISH GET OLD THEY COMPLAIN AND WHINE ABOUT EVERYTHING, AND CURSE THE FACT THAT THEIR LIVES HAVE BEEN WASTED.

I WANT TO KNOW IF LIFE IS SIMPLY ABOUT CIRCLING AROUND IN A SMALL PLACE UNTIL YOU BECOME OLD, OR IF THERE IS ANOTHER WAY TO LIVE IN THE WORLD?

MY DEAR CHILD, ARE YOU CRAZY? *WORLD?* ... *WORLD?* WHAT IS THIS OTHER *WORLD?* THE WORLD IS RIGHT HERE WHERE WE ARE. LIFE IS JUST AS THE ONE WE HAVE ...

JUST THEN, A LARGE FISH APPROACHED THEIR HOME.

NEIGHBOR, WHAT ARE YOU ARGUING ABOUT WITH YOUR CHILD? AREN'T YOU PLANNING TO GO SWIMMING TODAY?

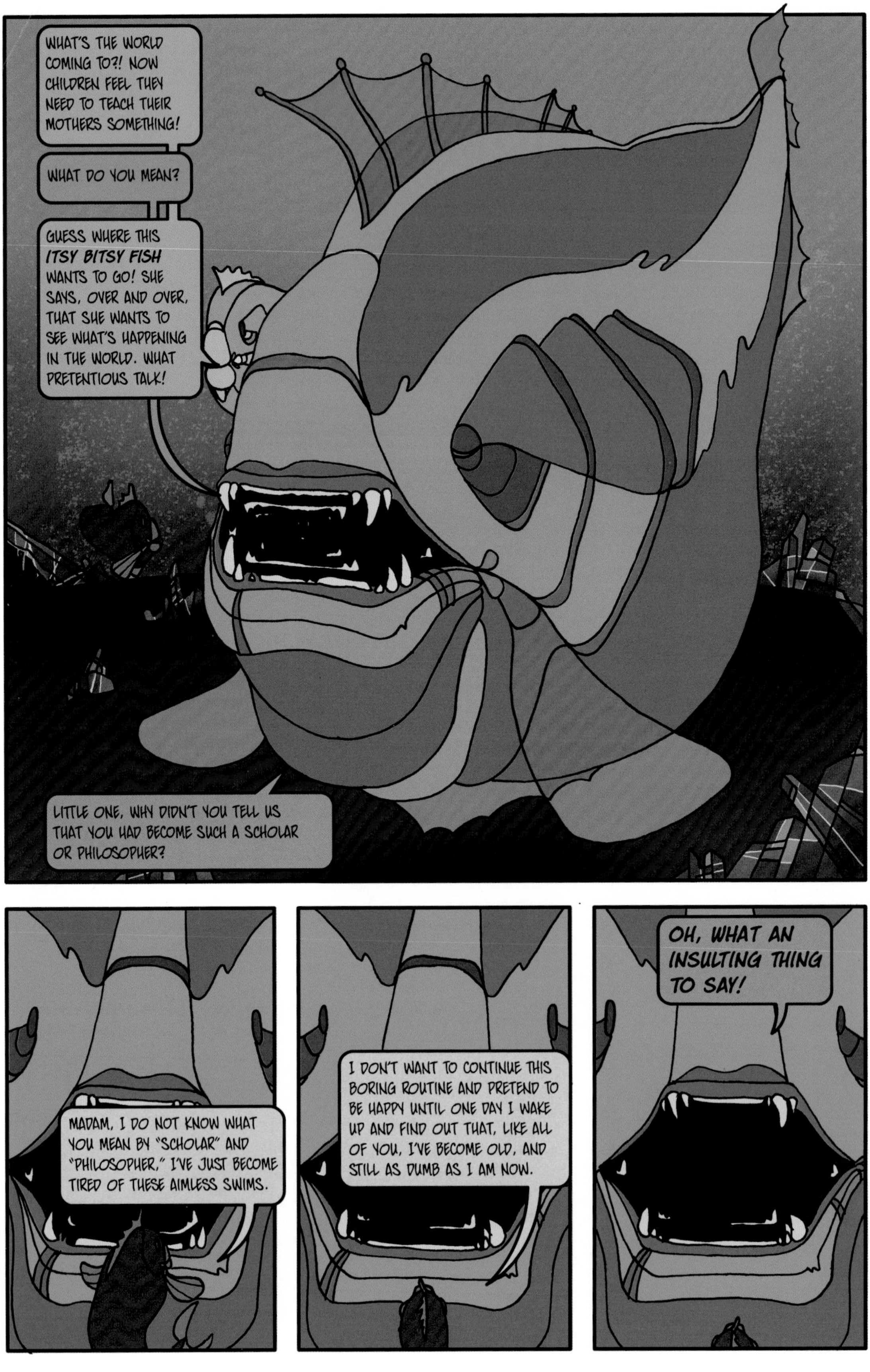
WHAT'S THE WORLD COMING TO?! NOW CHILDREN FEEL THEY NEED TO TEACH THEIR MOTHERS SOMETHING!
WHAT DO YOU MEAN?
GUESS WHERE THIS ITSY BITSY FISH WANTS TO GO! SHE SAYS, OVER AND OVER, THAT SHE WANTS TO SEE WHAT'S HAPPENING IN THE WORLD. WHAT PRETENTIOUS TALK!
LITTLE ONE, WHY DIDN'T YOU TELL US THAT YOU HAD BECOME SUCH A SCHOLAR OR PHILOSOPHER?
MADAM, I DO NOT KNOW WHAT YOU MEAN BY "SCHOLAR" AND "PHILOSOPHER," I'VE JUST BECOME TIRED OF THESE AIMLESS SWIMS.
I DON'T WANT TO CONTINUE THIS BORING ROUTINE AND PRETEND TO BE HAPPY UNTIL ONE DAY I WAKE UP AND FIND OUT THAT, LIKE ALL OF YOU, I'VE BECOME OLD, AND STILL AS DUMB AS I AM NOW.
OH, WHAT AN INSULTING THING TO SAY!

I NEVER THOUGHT THAT MY ONLY CHILD WOULD TURN OUT THIS WAY. WHAT EVIL PERSON PUT MY SWEET BABY UP TO THIS?

NO ONE PUT ME UP TO ANYTHING. I HAVE REASON AND INTELLIGENCE AND UNDERSTANDING. I HAVE EYES AND I CAN SEE.

SISTER, DO YOU REMEMBER THAT TWISTED-UP SNAIL?

YES, YOU'RE RIGHT. HE USED TO PUSH HIS IDEAS ON MY BABY. GOD KNOWS WHAT I SHOULD HAVE DONE TO HIM!

THAT'S ENOUGH, MOTHER. HE WAS MY FRIEND!

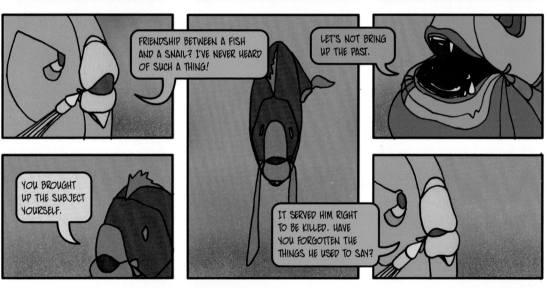

FRIENDSHIP BETWEEN A FISH AND A SNAIL? I'VE NEVER HEARD OF SUCH A THING!

LET'S NOT BRING UP THE PAST.

YOU BROUGHT UP THE SUBJECT YOURSELF.

IT SERVED HIM RIGHT TO BE KILLED. HAVE YOU FORGOTTEN THE THINGS HE USED TO SAY?

THE ARGUING VOICES ATTRACTED THE OTHER FISH.

THEN, KILL ME TOO, SINCE I SAY THE VERY SAME THINGS.

MADAM, IF YOU DON'T RAISE YOUR CHILD CORRECTLY, YOU SHOULD BE PREPARED FOR THE CONSEQUENCES.

DID YOU THINK WE'D SPARE YOU?

GO AWAY. DON'T YOU TOUCH MY CHILD.

LET'S DO TO THE LITTLE FISH WHAT WE DID TO THE OLD SNAIL—BEFORE SHE GETS INTO TROUBLE.

I'M ASHAMED TO LIVE NEXT TO YOU.

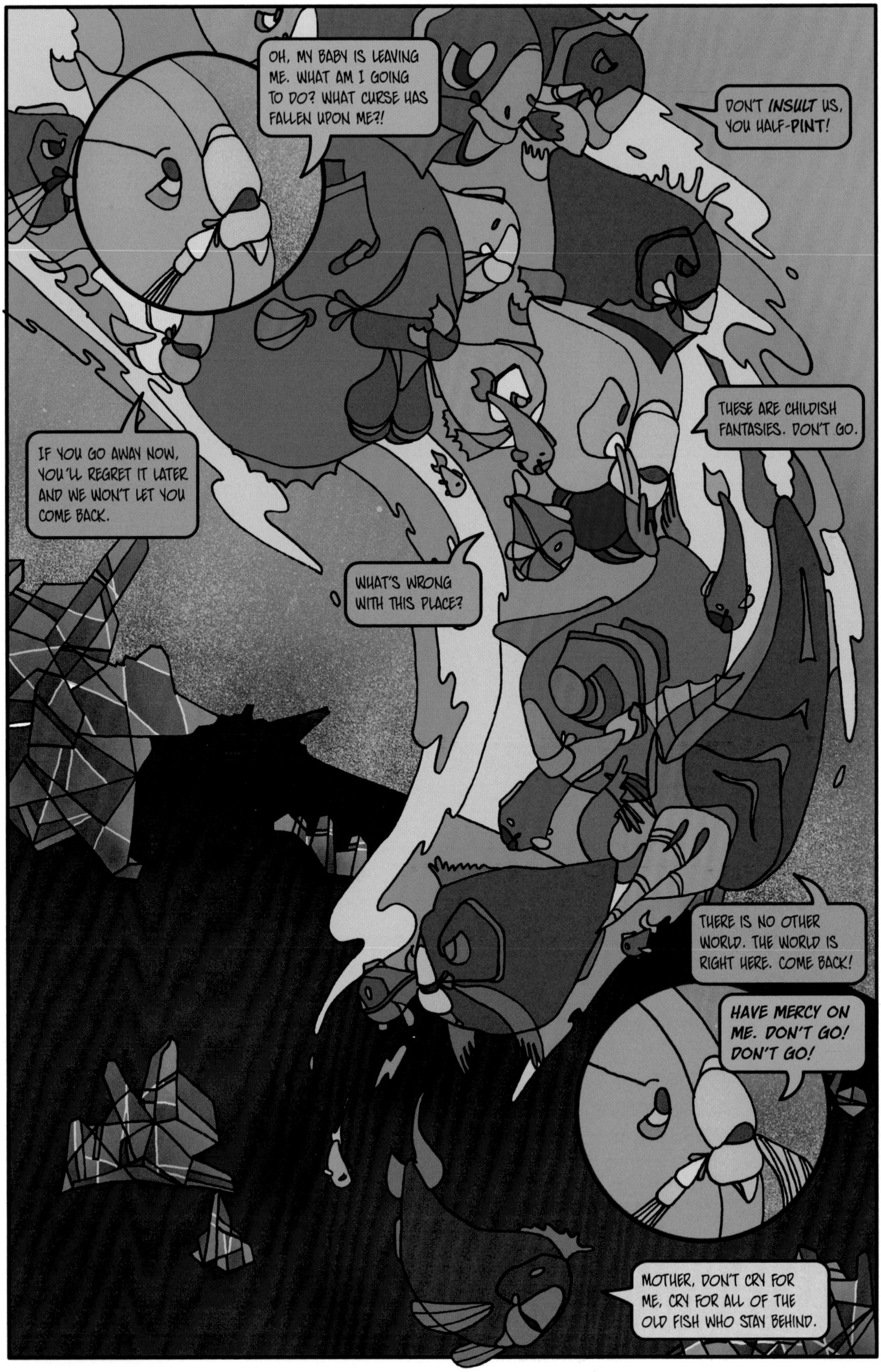
OH, MY BABY IS LEAVING ME. WHAT AM I GOING TO DO? WHAT CURSE HAS FALLEN UPON ME?!
DON'T INSULT US, YOU HALF-PINT!
THESE ARE CHILDISH FANTASIES. DON'T GO.
IF YOU GO AWAY NOW, YOU'LL REGRET IT LATER AND WE WON'T LET YOU COME BACK.
WHAT'S WRONG WITH THIS PLACE?
THERE IS NO OTHER WORLD. THE WORLD IS RIGHT HERE. COME BACK!
HAVE MERCY ON ME. DON'T GO! DON'T GO!
MOTHER, DON'T CRY FOR ME, CRY FOR ALL OF THE OLD FISH WHO STAY BEHIND.

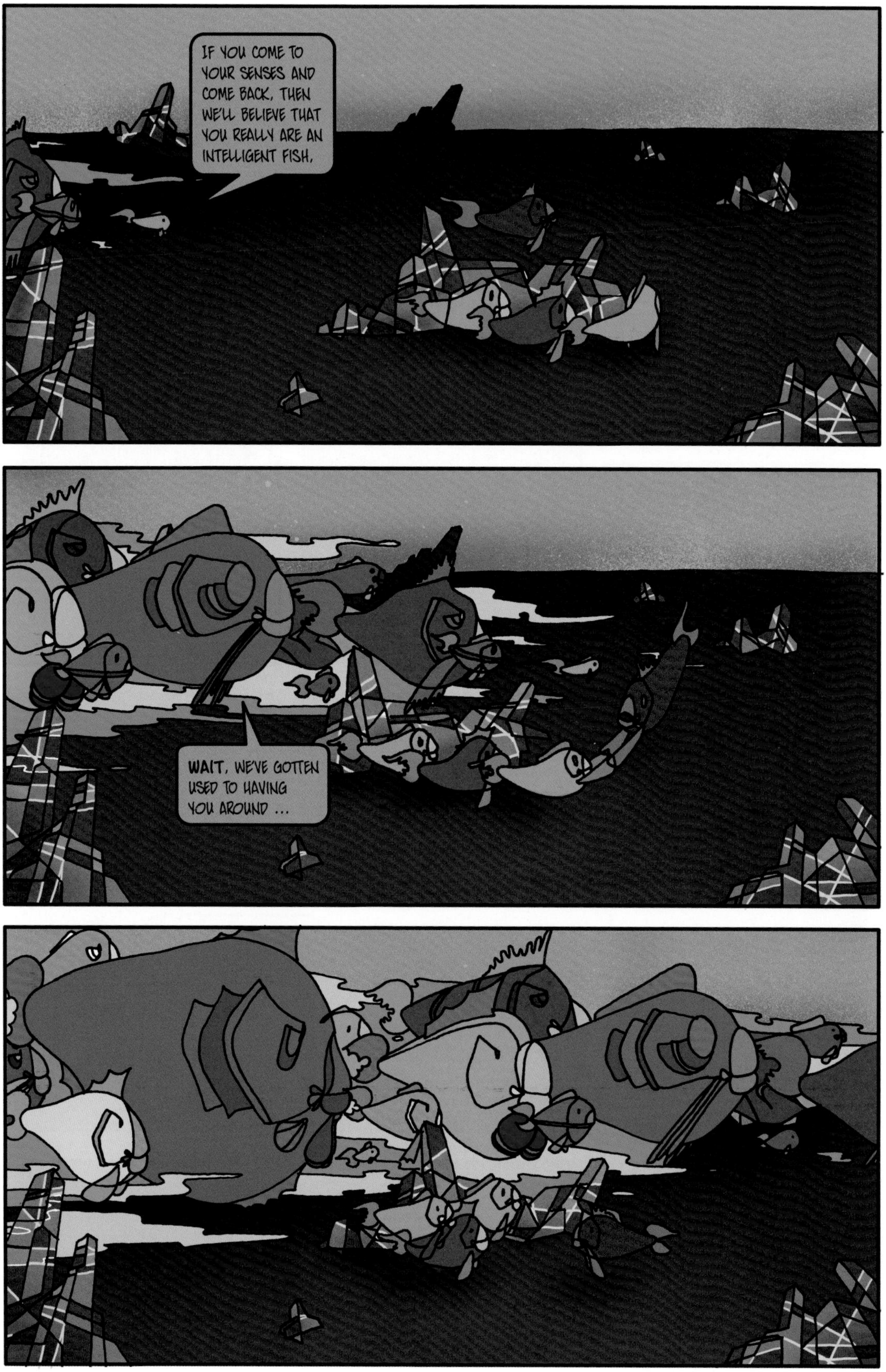
IF YOU COME TO YOUR SENSES AND COME BACK, THEN WE'LL BELIEVE THAT YOU REALLY ARE AN INTELLIGENT FISH.
WAIT, WE'VE GOTTEN USED TO HAVING YOU AROUND ...

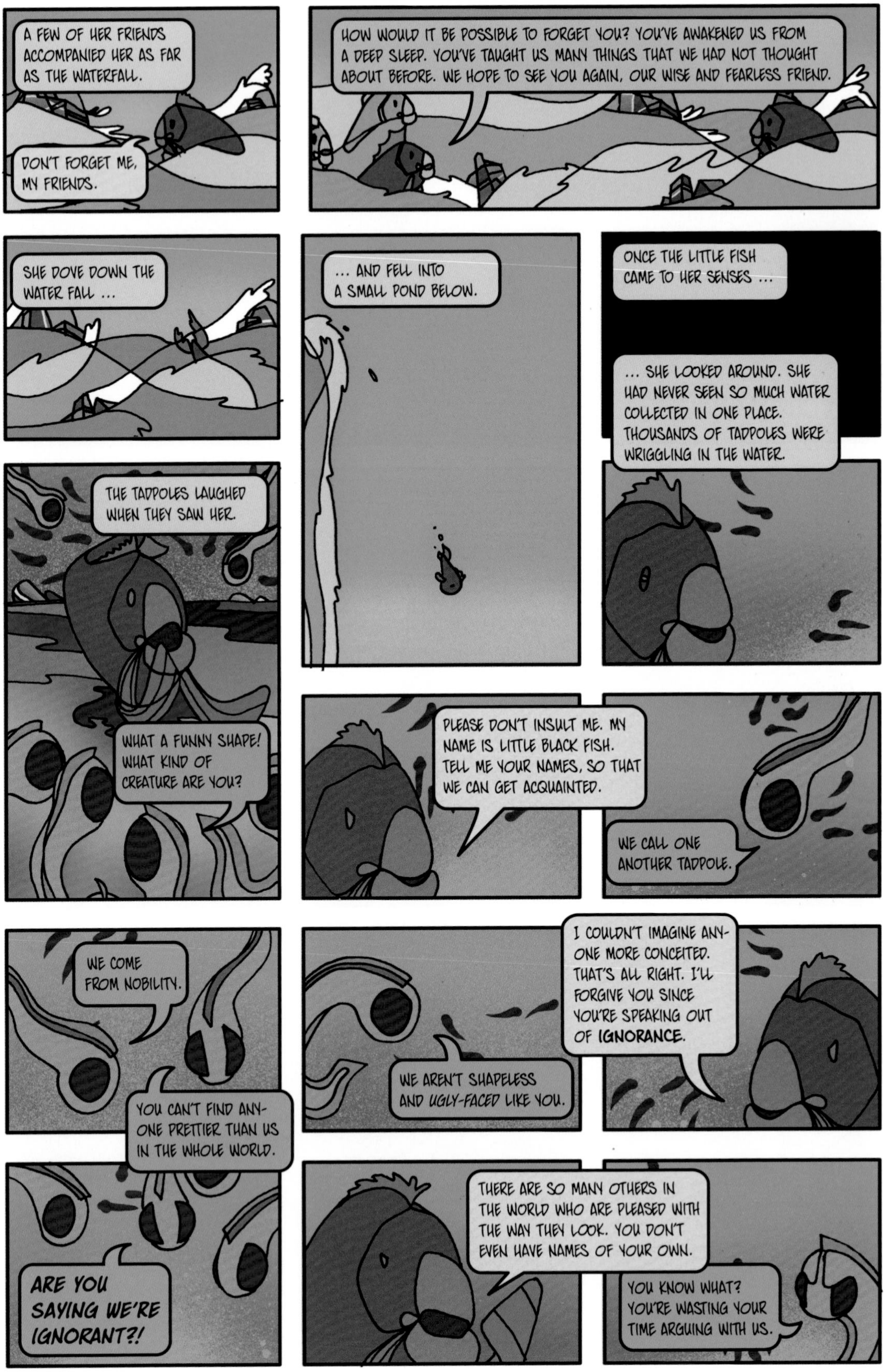
A FEW OF HER FRIENDS ACCOMPANIED HER AS FAR AS THE WATERFALL.
DON'T FORGET ME, MY FRIENDS.
HOW WOULD IT BE POSSIBLE TO FORGET YOU? YOU'VE AWAKENED US FROM A DEEP SLEEP. YOU'VE TAUGHT US MANY THINGS THAT WE HAD NOT THOUGHT ABOUT BEFORE. WE HOPE TO SEE YOU AGAIN, OUR WISE AND FEARLESS FRIEND.
SHE DOVE DOWN THE WATER FALL ...
... AND FELL INTO A SMALL POND BELOW.
ONCE THE LITTLE FISH CAME TO HER SENSES ...
... SHE LOOKED AROUND. SHE HAD NEVER SEEN SO MUCH WATER COLLECTED IN ONE PLACE. THOUSANDS OF TADPOLES WERE WRIGGLING IN THE WATER.
THE TADPOLES LAUGHED WHEN THEY SAW HER.
WHAT A FUNNY SHAPE! WHAT KIND OF CREATURE ARE YOU?
PLEASE DON'T INSULT ME. MY NAME IS LITTLE BLACK FISH. TELL ME YOUR NAMES, SO THAT WE CAN GET ACQUAINTED.
WE CALL ONE ANOTHER TADPOLE.
WE COME FROM NOBILITY.
YOU CAN'T FIND ANY-ONE PRETTIER THAN US IN THE WHOLE WORLD.
WE AREN'T SHAPELESS AND UGLY-FACED LIKE YOU.
I COULDN'T IMAGINE ANY-ONE MORE CONCEITED. THAT'S ALL RIGHT. I'LL FORGIVE YOU SINCE YOU'RE SPEAKING OUT OF IGNORANCE.
ARE YOU SAYING WE'RE IGNORANT?!
THERE ARE SO MANY OTHERS IN THE WORLD WHO ARE PLEASED WITH THE WAY THEY LOOK. YOU DON'T EVEN HAVE NAMES OF YOUR OWN.
YOU KNOW WHAT? YOU'RE WASTING YOUR TIME ARGUING WITH US.

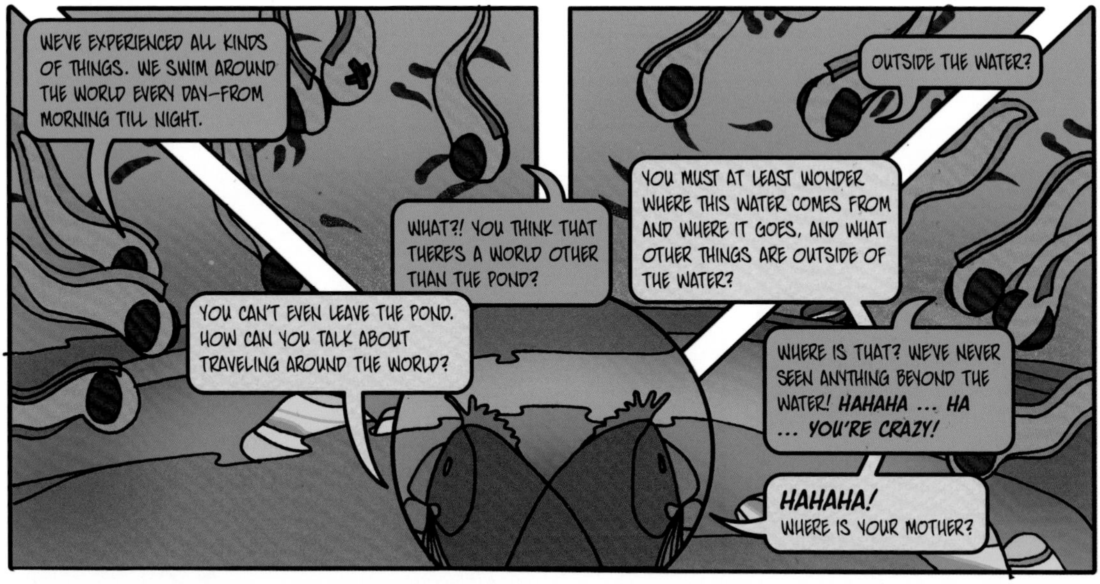
WE'VE EXPERIENCED ALL KINDS OF THINGS. WE SWIM AROUND THE WORLD EVERY DAY—FROM MORNING TILL NIGHT.
WHAT?! YOU THINK THAT THERE'S A WORLD OTHER THAN THE POND?
YOU CAN'T EVEN LEAVE THE POND. HOW CAN YOU TALK ABOUT TRAVELING AROUND THE WORLD?
OUTSIDE THE WATER?
YOU MUST AT LEAST WONDER WHERE THIS WATER COMES FROM AND WHERE IT GOES, AND WHAT OTHER THINGS ARE OUTSIDE OF THE WATER?
WHERE IS THAT? WE'VE NEVER SEEN ANYTHING BEYOND THE WATER! HAHAHA ... HA ... YOU'RE CRAZY!
HAHAHA! WHERE IS YOUR MOTHER?

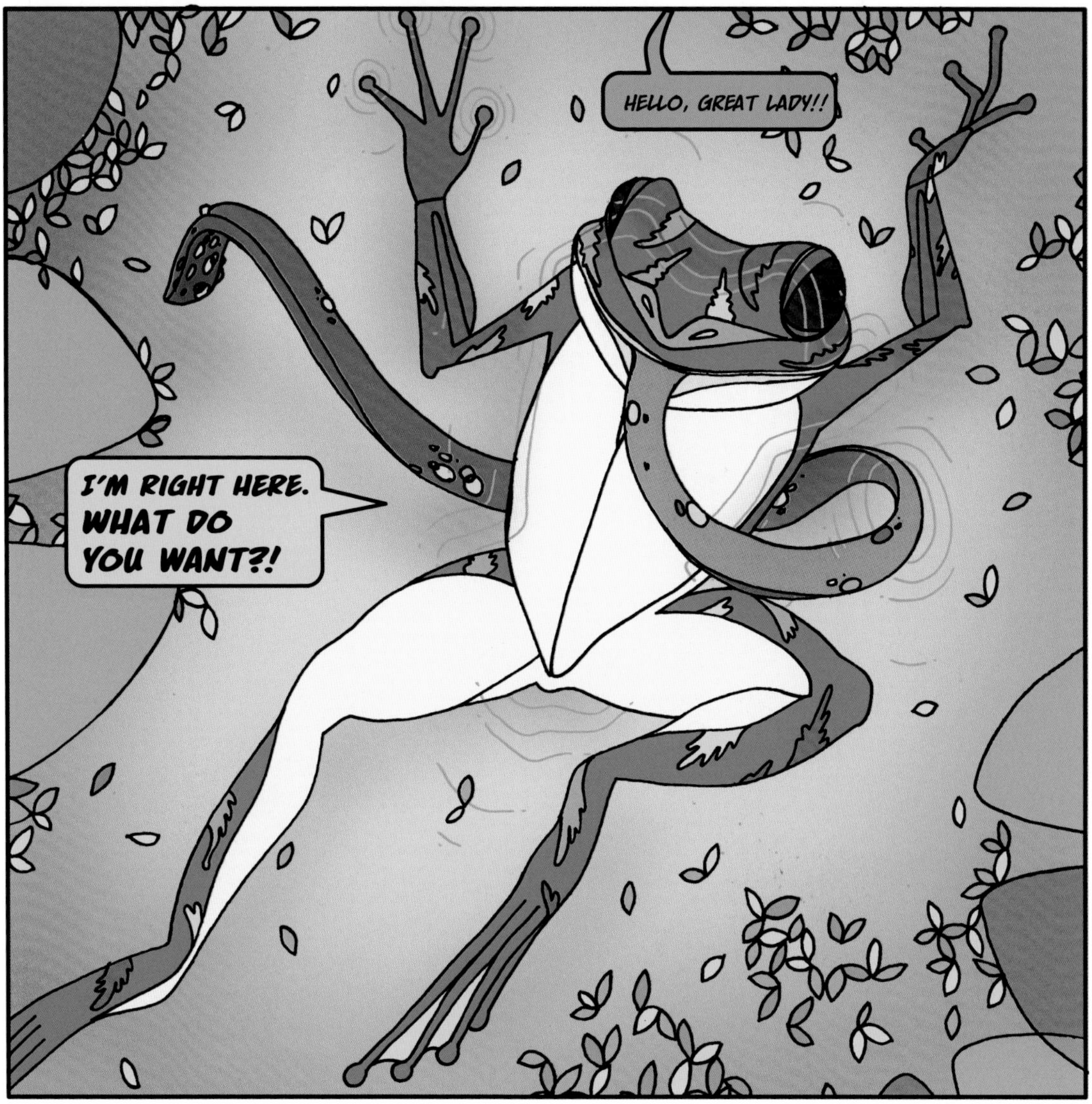
HELLO, GREAT LADY!!
I'M RIGHT HERE. WHAT DO YOU WANT?!

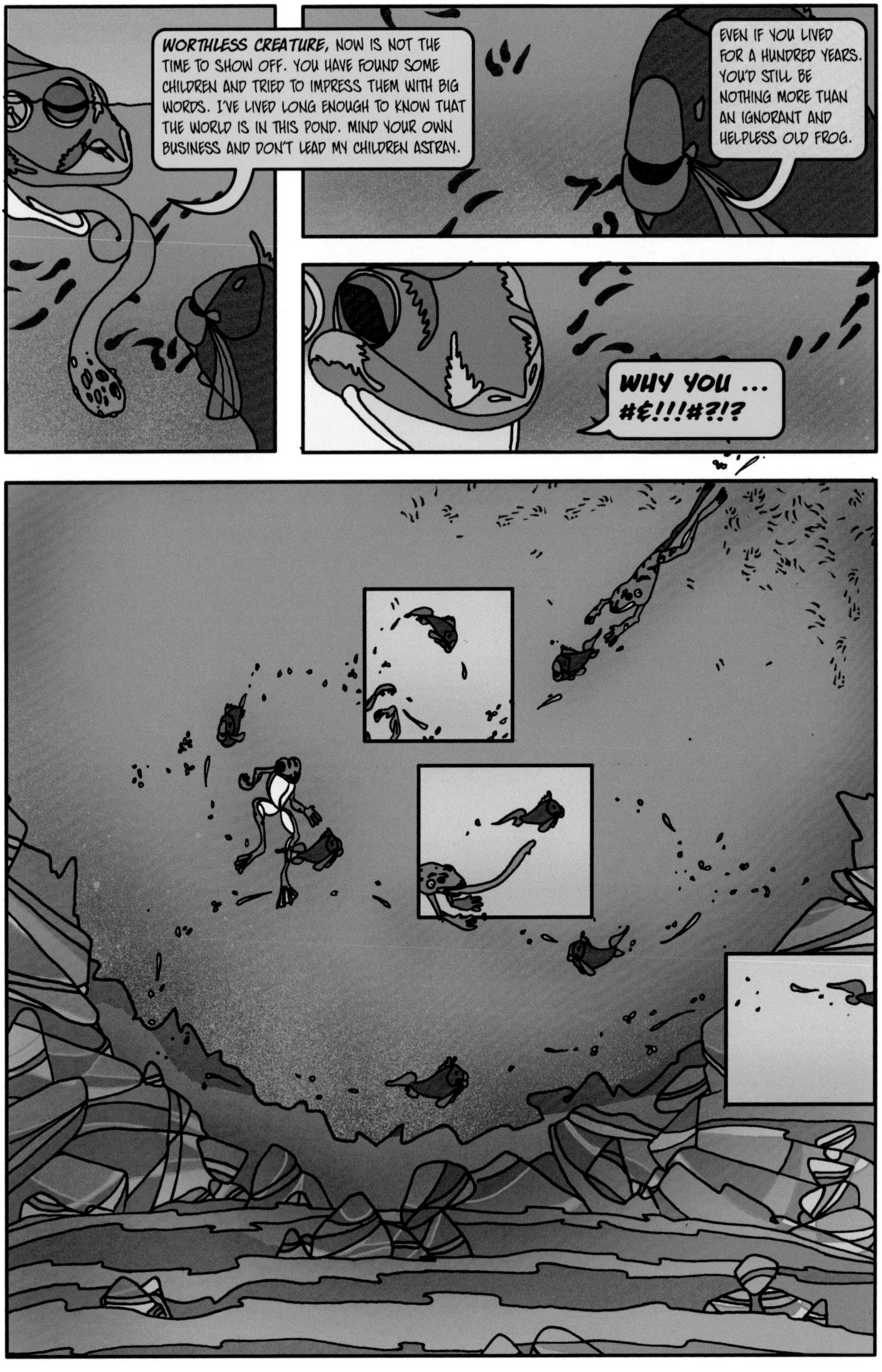
WORTHLESS CREATURE, NOW IS NOT THE TIME TO SHOW OFF. YOU HAVE FOUND SOME CHILDREN AND TRIED TO IMPRESS THEM WITH BIG WORDS. I'VE LIVED LONG ENOUGH TO KNOW THAT THE WORLD IS IN THIS POND. MIND YOUR OWN BUSINESS AND DON'T LEAD MY CHILDREN ASTRAY.
EVEN IF YOU LIVED FOR A HUNDRED YEARS. YOU'D STILL BE NOTHING MORE THAN AN IGNORANT AND HELPLESS OLD FROG.
WHY YOU ... #€!!!#?!?

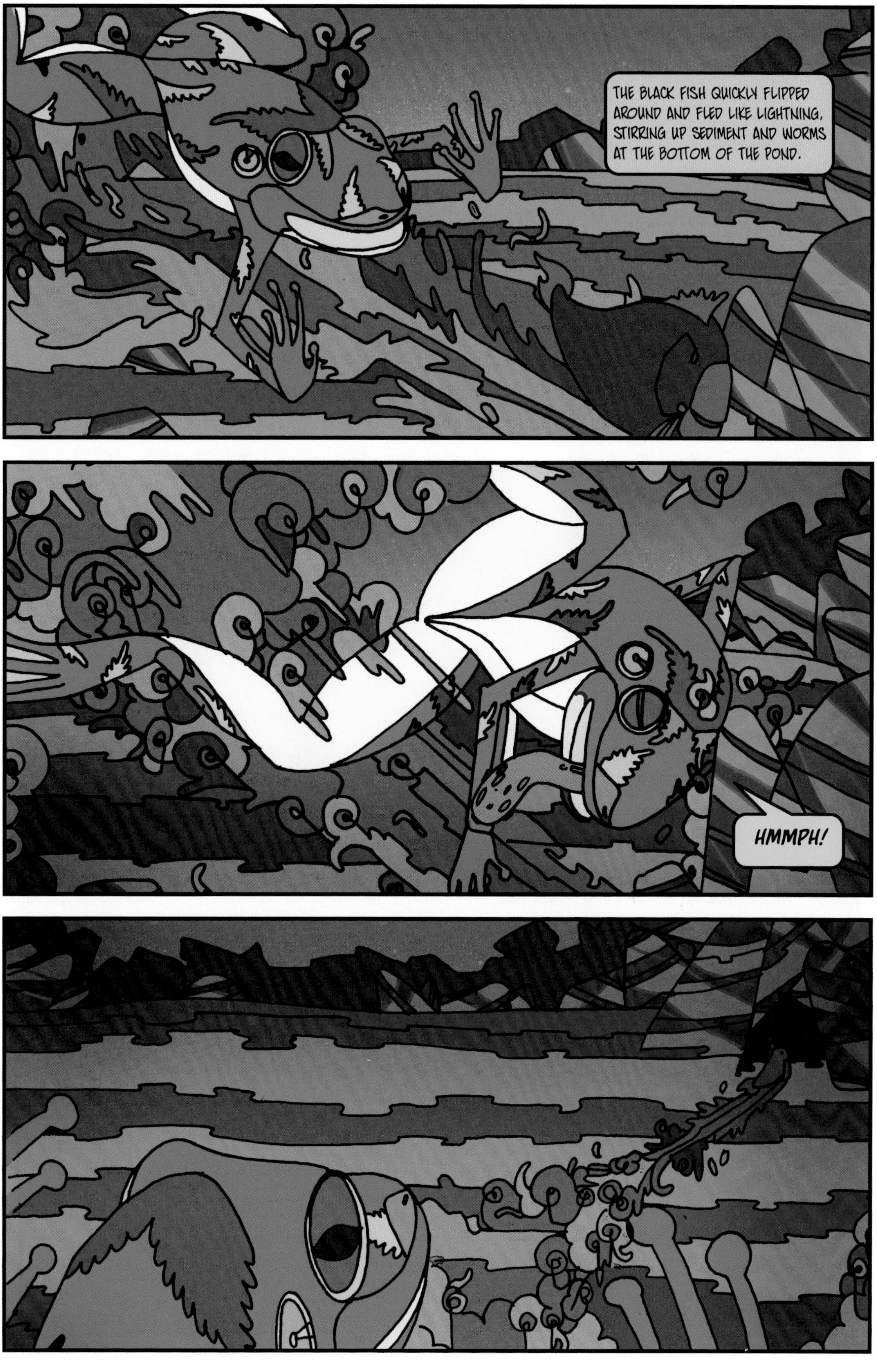
THE BLACK FISH QUICKLY FLIPPED AROUND AND FLED LIKE LIGHTNING, STIRRING UP SEDIMENT AND WORMS AT THE BOTTOM OF THE POND.
HMMPH!

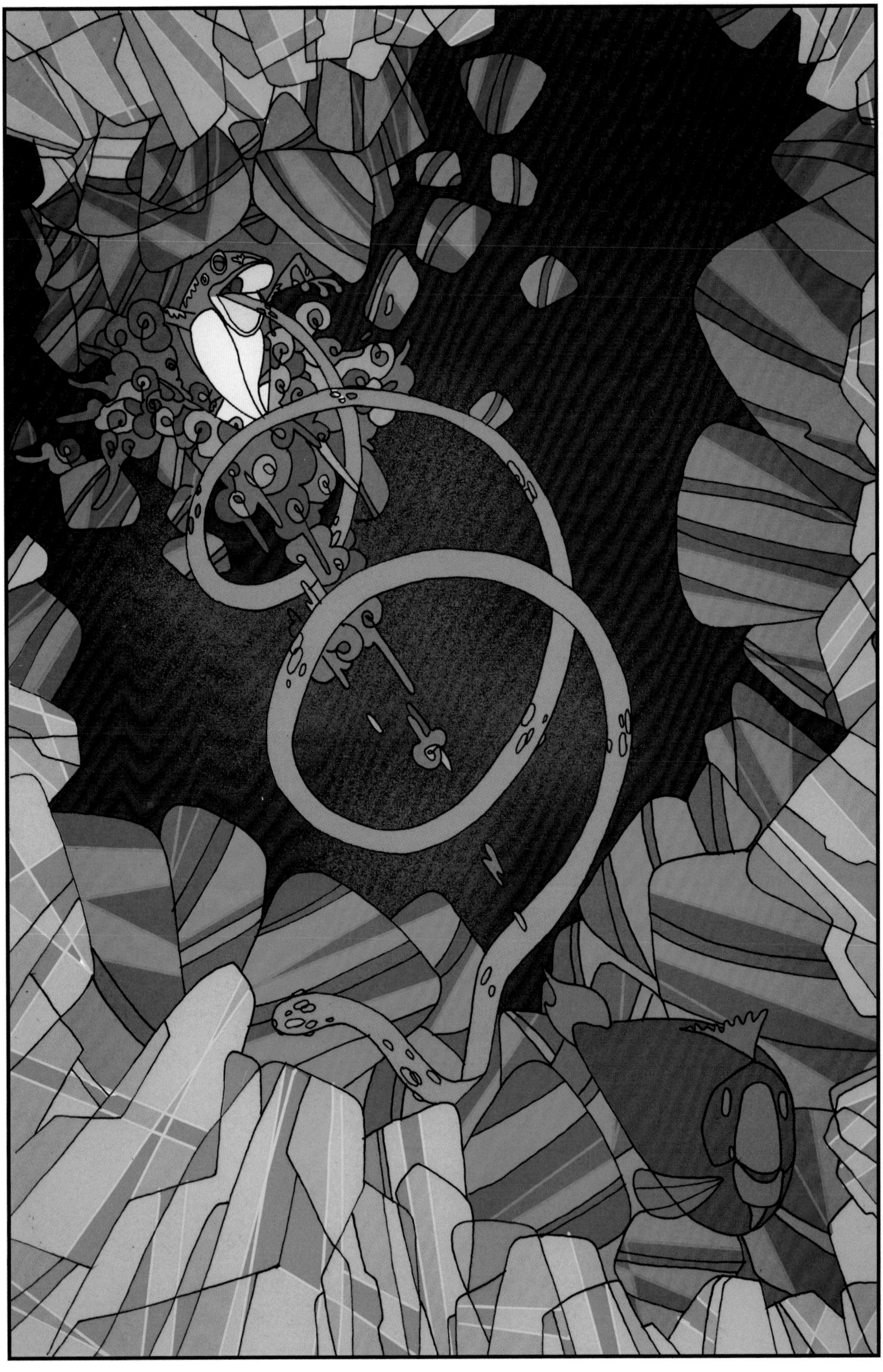

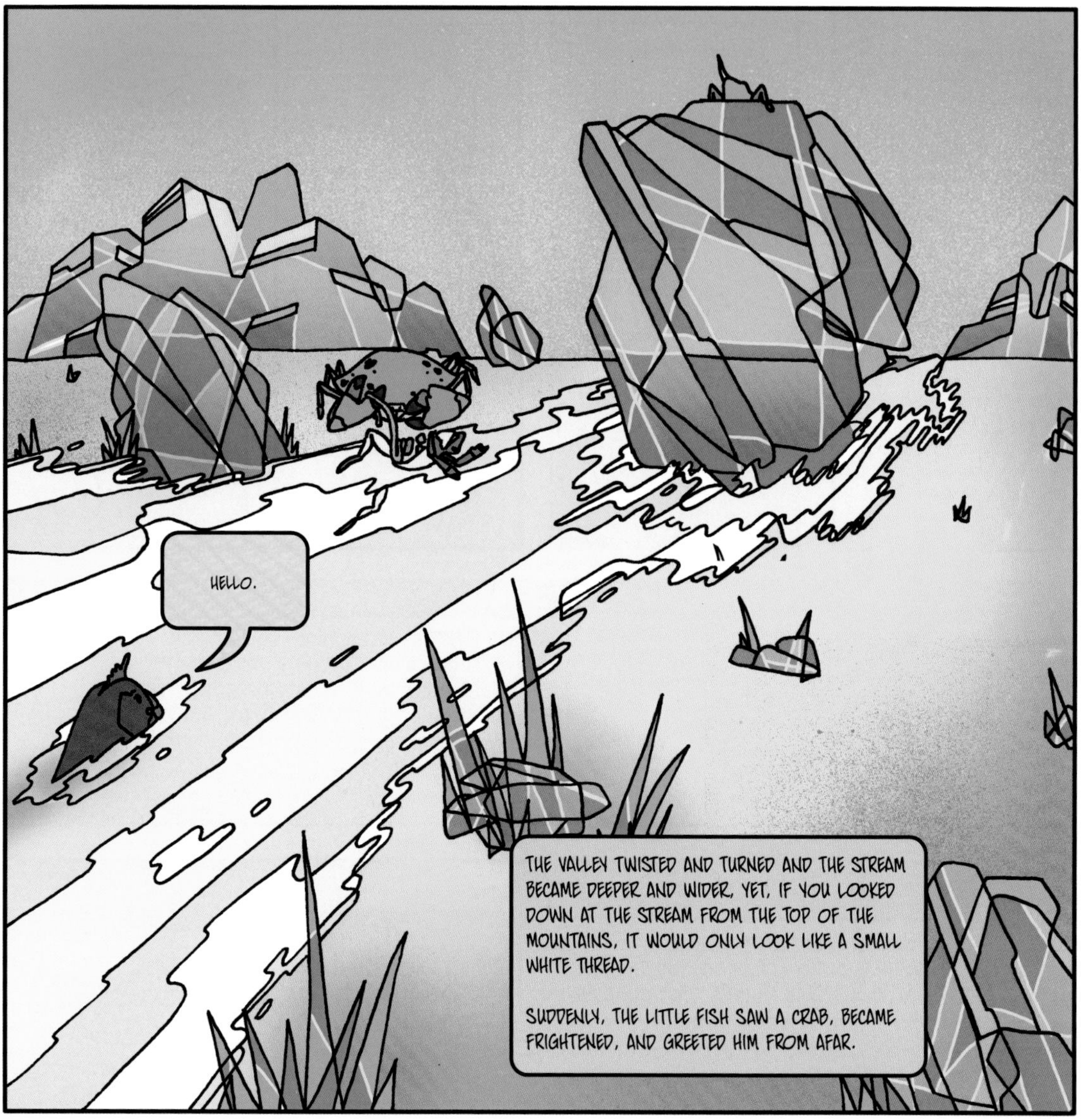
HELLO.
THE VALLEY TWISTED AND TURNED AND THE STREAM BECAME DEEPER AND WIDER, YET, IF YOU LOOKED DOWN AT THE STREAM FROM THE TOP OF THE MOUNTAINS, IT WOULD ONLY LOOK LIKE A SMALL WHITE THREAD.
SUDDENLY, THE LITTLE FISH SAW A CRAB, BECAME FRIGHTENED, AND GREETED HIM FROM AFAR.

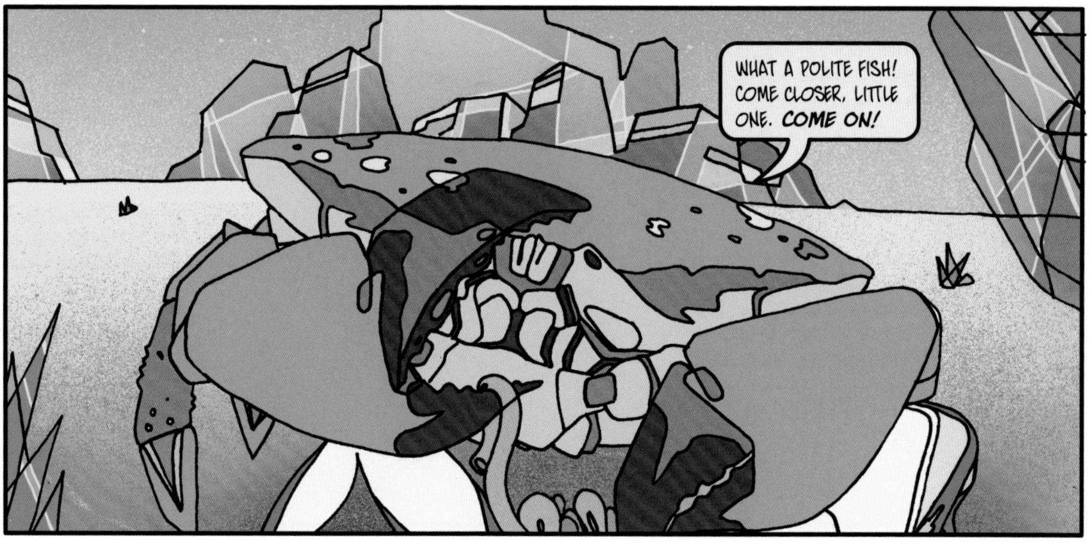
WHAT A POLITE FISH! COME CLOSER, LITTLE ONE. **COME ON!**

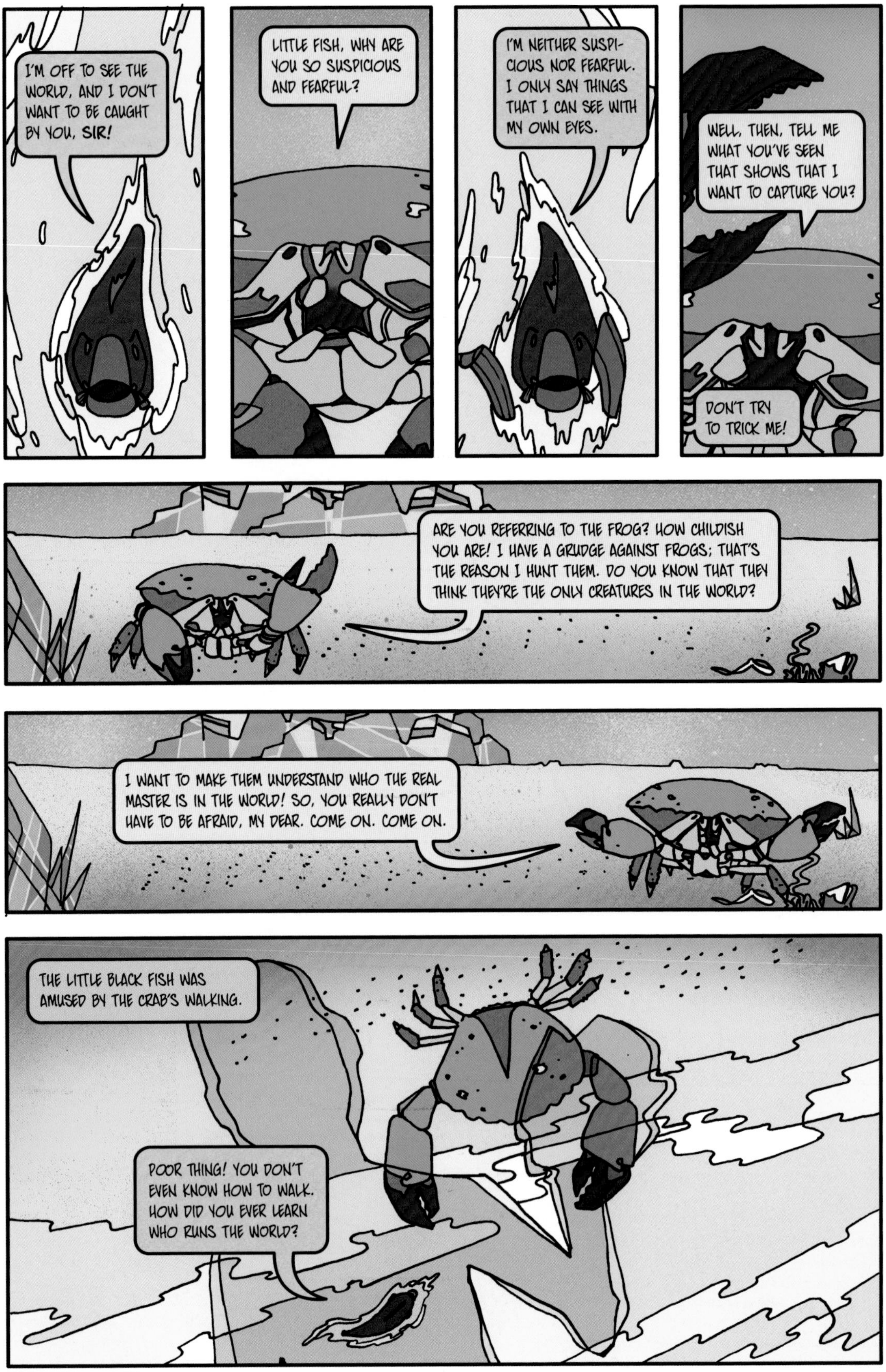
I'M OFF TO SEE THE WORLD, AND I DON'T WANT TO BE CAUGHT BY YOU, SIR!
LITTLE FISH, WHY ARE YOU SO SUSPICIOUS AND FEARFUL?
I'M NEITHER SUSPICIOUS NOR FEARFUL. I ONLY SAY THINGS THAT I CAN SEE WITH MY OWN EYES.
WELL, THEN, TELL ME WHAT YOU'VE SEEN THAT SHOWS THAT I WANT TO CAPTURE YOU?
DON'T TRY TO TRICK ME!
ARE YOU REFERRING TO THE FROG? HOW CHILDISH YOU ARE! I HAVE A GRUDGE AGAINST FROGS; THAT'S THE REASON I HUNT THEM. DO YOU KNOW THAT THEY THINK THEY'RE THE ONLY CREATURES IN THE WORLD?
I WANT TO MAKE THEM UNDERSTAND WHO THE REAL MASTER IS IN THE WORLD! SO, YOU REALLY DON'T HAVE TO BE AFRAID, MY DEAR. COME ON. COME ON.
THE LITTLE BLACK FISH WAS AMUSED BY THE CRAB'S WALKING.
POOR THING! YOU DON'T EVEN KNOW HOW TO WALK. HOW DID YOU EVER LEARN WHO RUNS THE WORLD?

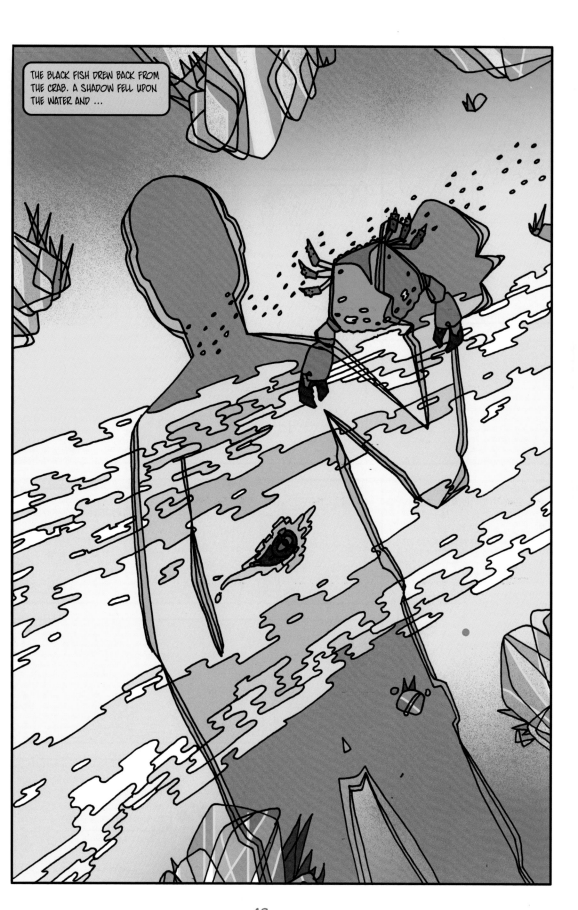

THE BLACK FISH DREW BACK FROM THE CRAB. A SHADOW FELL UPON THE WATER AND ...

19

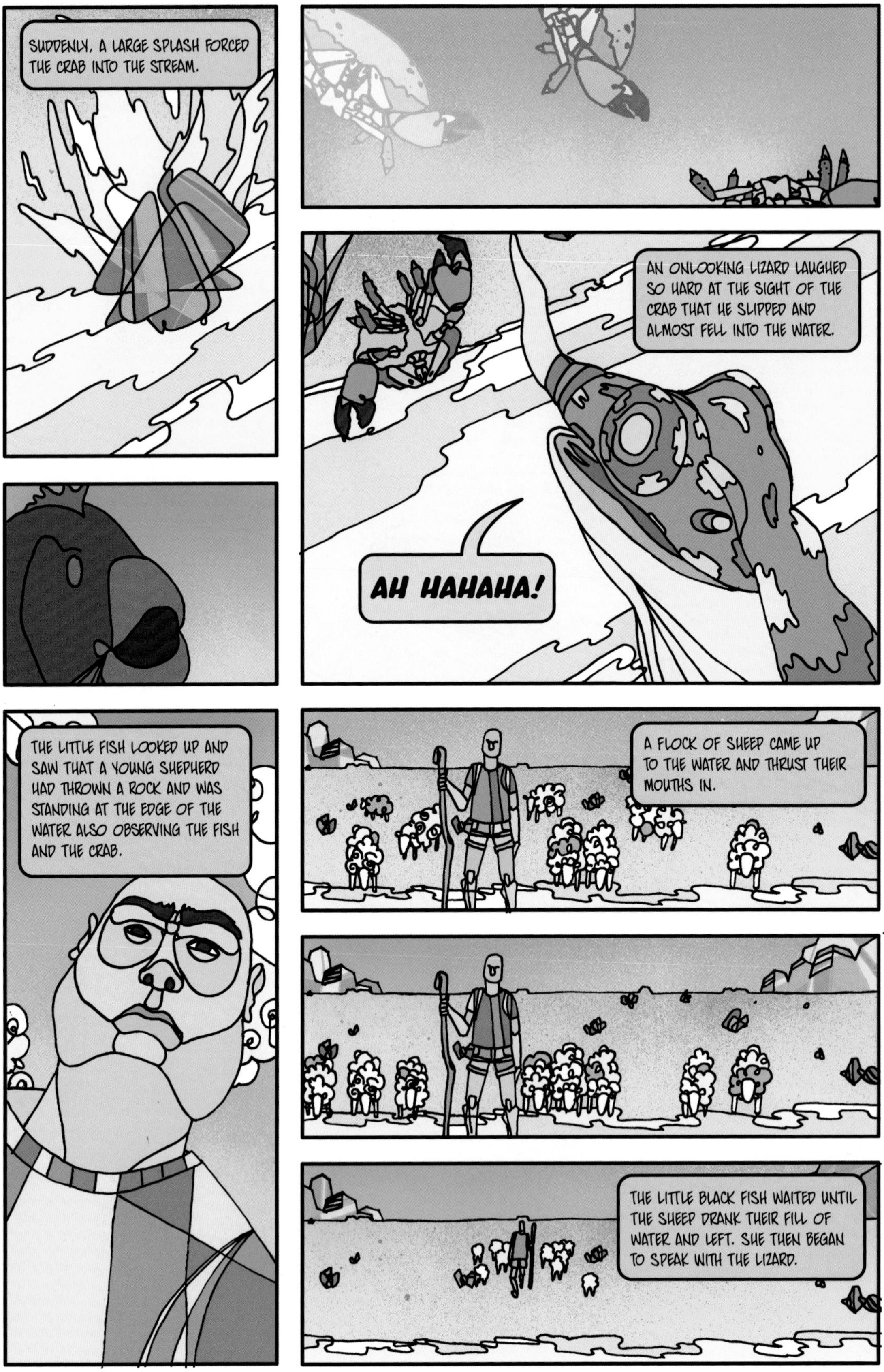

SUDDENLY, A LARGE SPLASH FORCED THE CRAB INTO THE STREAM.
AN ONLOOKING LIZARD LAUGHED SO HARD AT THE SIGHT OF THE CRAB THAT HE SLIPPED AND ALMOST FELL INTO THE WATER.
AH HAHAHA!
THE LITTLE FISH LOOKED UP AND SAW THAT A YOUNG SHEPHERD HAD THROWN A ROCK AND WAS STANDING AT THE EDGE OF THE WATER ALSO OBSERVING THE FISH AND THE CRAB.
A FLOCK OF SHEEP CAME UP TO THE WATER AND THRUST THEIR MOUTHS IN.
THE LITTLE BLACK FISH WAITED UNTIL THE SHEEP DRANK THEIR FILL OF WATER AND LEFT. SHE THEN BEGAN TO SPEAK WITH THE LIZARD.

DEAR LIZARD, I'M THE LITTLE BLACK FISH WHO IS IN SEARCH OF THE END OF THE STREAM.

YOU SEEM WISE. MAY I ASK YOU SOMETHING?

ASK ANYTHING YOU WANT.

ALL ALONG THE WAY, OTHERS HAVE BEEN FRIGHTENING ME A GREAT DEAL. DO YOU KNOW ANYTHING ABOUT THE PELICAN, THE SWORDFISH AND THE HERON??

THE SWORDFISH, AND THE HERON AREN'T FOUND IN THIS AREA, ESPECIALLY THE SWORDFISH WHO LIVES IN THE SEA.

BUT THE PELICAN COULD BE LURKING SOMEWHERE. BE CAREFUL AND MAKE SURE THAT HE DOESN'T TRICK YOU AND CATCH YOU IN HIS POUCH.

WHAT POUCH?

UNDER HIS THROAT, THE PELICAN HAS A POUCH THAT HOLDS A LOT OF WATER.

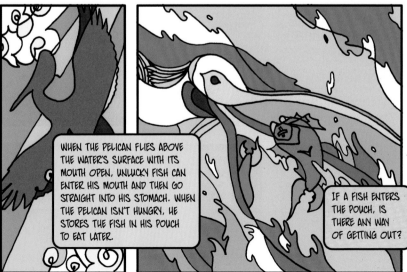

WHEN THE PELICAN FLIES ABOVE THE WATER'S SURFACE WITH ITS MOUTH OPEN, UNLUCKY FISH CAN ENTER HIS MOUTH AND THEN GO STRAIGHT INTO HIS STOMACH. WHEN THE PELICAN ISN'T HUNGRY, HE STORES THE FISH IN HIS POUCH TO EAT LATER.

IF A FISH ENTERS THE POUCH, IS THERE ANY WAY OF GETTING OUT?

THERE IS NO WAY UNLESS, PERHAPS, THE FISH WAS ABLE TO RIP OPEN THE POUCH AND JUMP OUT.

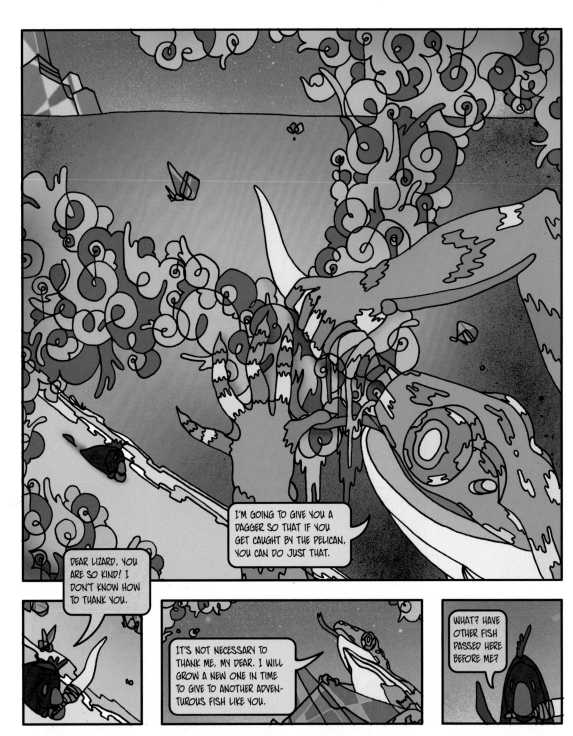

I'M GOING TO GIVE YOU A DAGGER SO THAT IF YOU GET CAUGHT BY THE PELICAN, YOU CAN DO JUST THAT.

DEAR LIZARD, YOU ARE SO KIND! I DON'T KNOW HOW TO THANK YOU.

IT'S NOT NECESSARY TO THANK ME, MY DEAR. I WILL GROW A NEW ONE IN TIME TO GIVE TO ANOTHER ADVENTUROUS FISH LIKE YOU.

WHAT? HAVE OTHER FISH PASSED HERE BEFORE ME?

MANY HAVE PASSED BY. THEY FORM THEMSELVES INTO A BIG GROUP AND GIVE THE FISHERMAN A HARD TIME.

EXCUSE ME IF YOU THINK THAT I AM BEING NOSEY, BUT WOULD YOU TELL ME HOW?

VERY CAREFULLY.

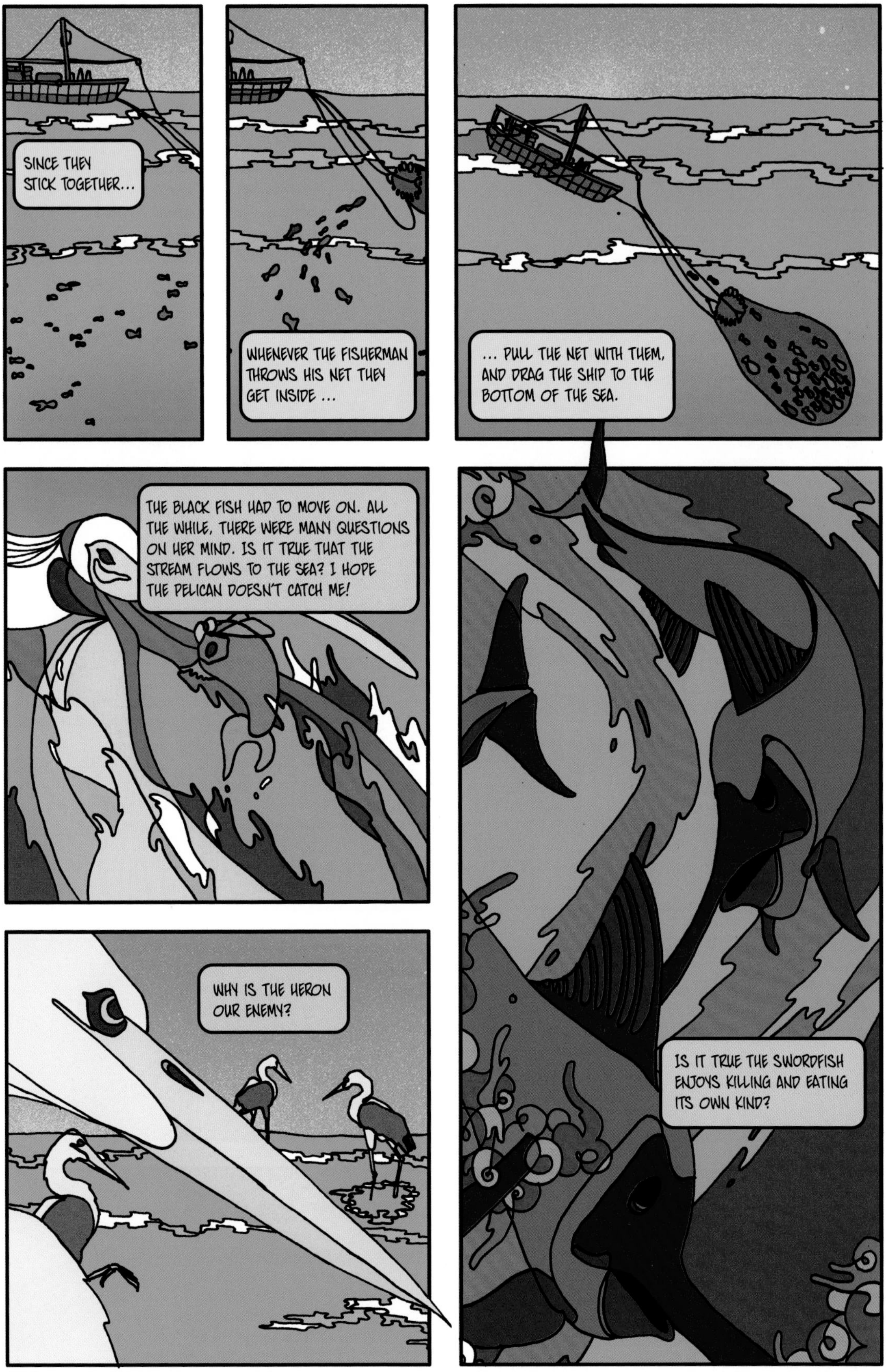
SINCE THEY STICK TOGETHER...
WHENEVER THE FISHERMAN THROWS HIS NET THEY GET INSIDE ...
... PULL THE NET WITH THEM, AND DRAG THE SHIP TO THE BOTTOM OF THE SEA.
THE BLACK FISH HAD TO MOVE ON. ALL THE WHILE, THERE WERE MANY QUESTIONS ON HER MIND. IS IT TRUE THAT THE STREAM FLOWS TO THE SEA? I HOPE THE PELICAN DOESN'T CATCH ME!
IS IT TRUE THE SWORDFISH ENJOYS KILLING AND EATING ITS OWN KIND?
WHY IS THE HERON OUR ENEMY?

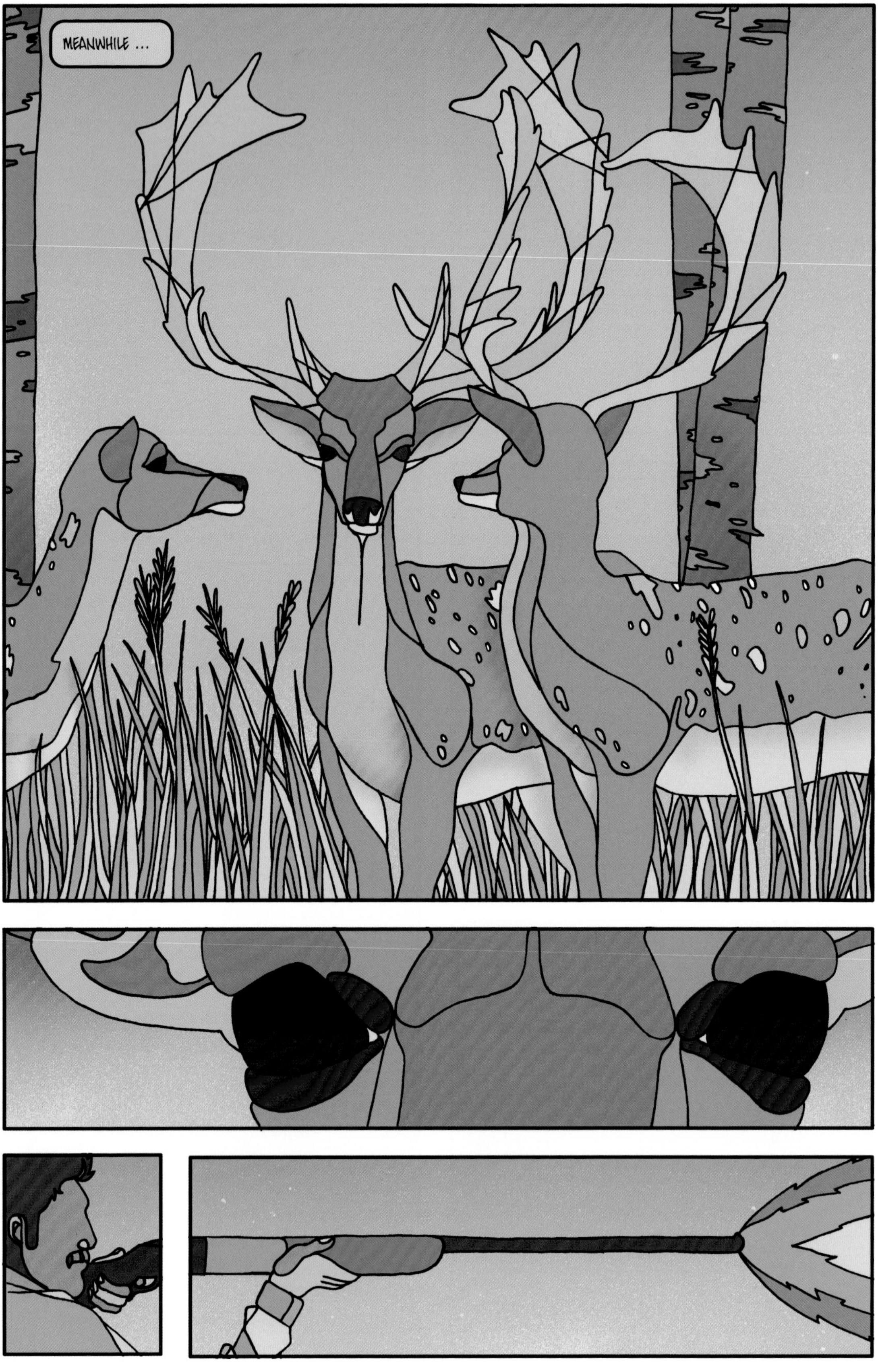
MEANWHILE ...

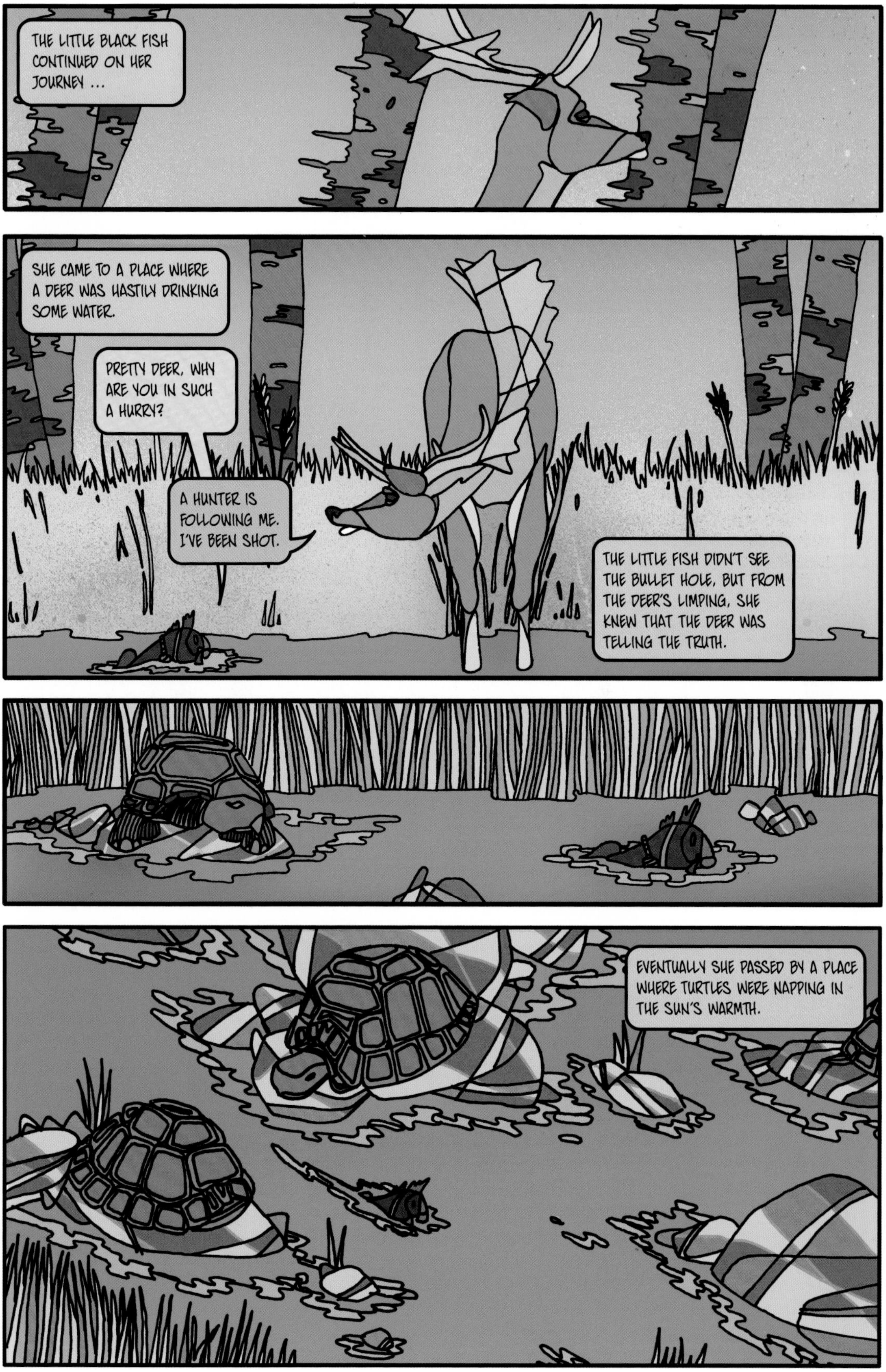
THE LITTLE BLACK FISH CONTINUED ON HER JOURNEY ...
SHE CAME TO A PLACE WHERE A DEER WAS HASTILY DRINKING SOME WATER.
PRETTY DEER, WHY ARE YOU IN SUCH A HURRY?
A HUNTER IS FOLLOWING ME. I'VE BEEN SHOT.
THE LITTLE FISH DIDN'T SEE THE BULLET HOLE, BUT FROM THE DEER'S LIMPING, SHE KNEW THAT THE DEER WAS TELLING THE TRUTH.
EVENTUALLY SHE PASSED BY A PLACE WHERE TURTLES WERE NAPPING IN THE SUN'S WARMTH.

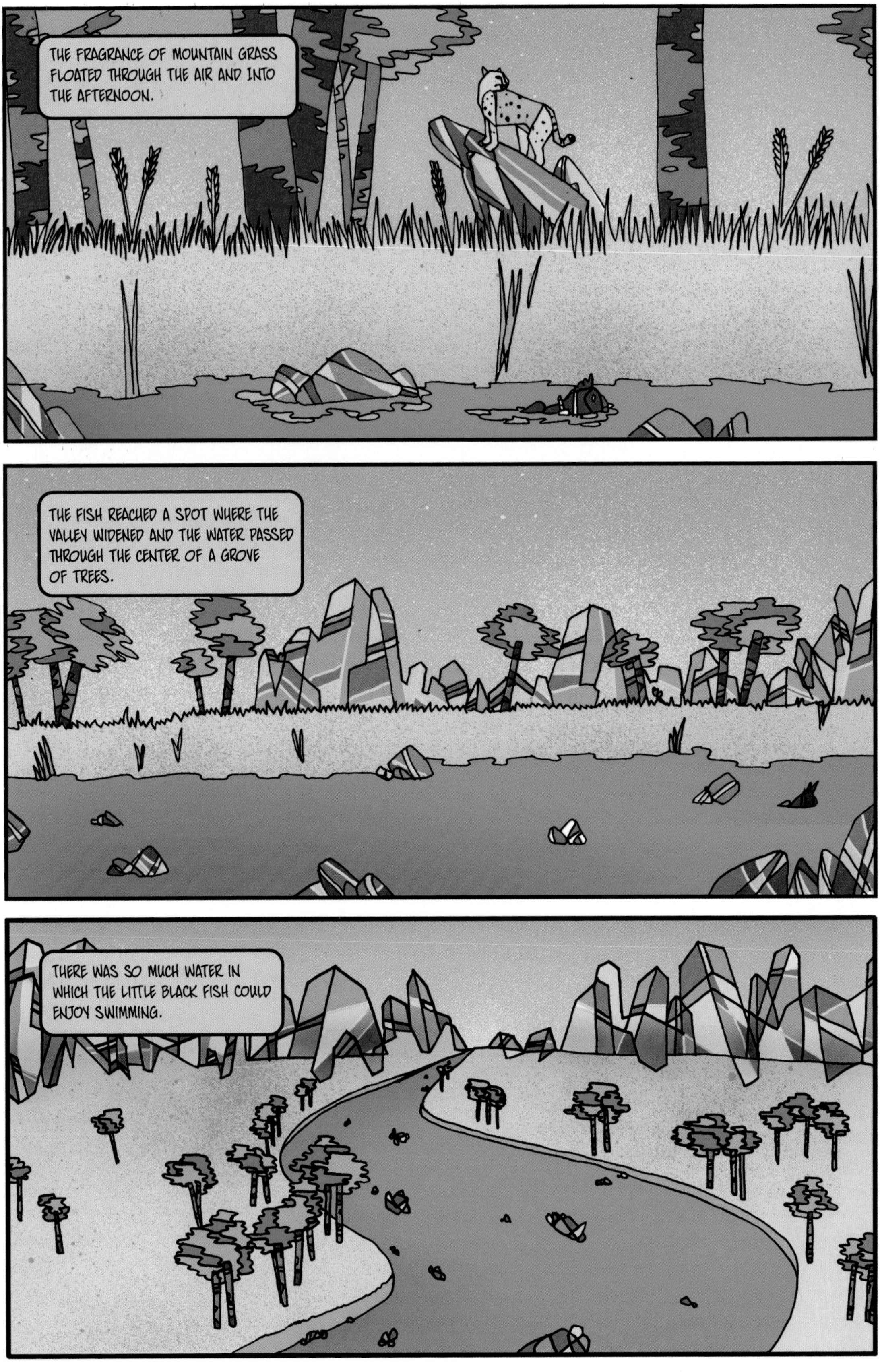
THE FRAGRANCE OF MOUNTAIN GRASS FLOATED THROUGH THE AIR AND INTO THE AFTERNOON.
THE FISH REACHED A SPOT WHERE THE VALLEY WIDENED AND THE WATER PASSED THROUGH THE CENTER OF A GROVE OF TREES.
THERE WAS SO MUCH WATER IN WHICH THE LITTLE BLACK FISH COULD ENJOY SWIMMING.

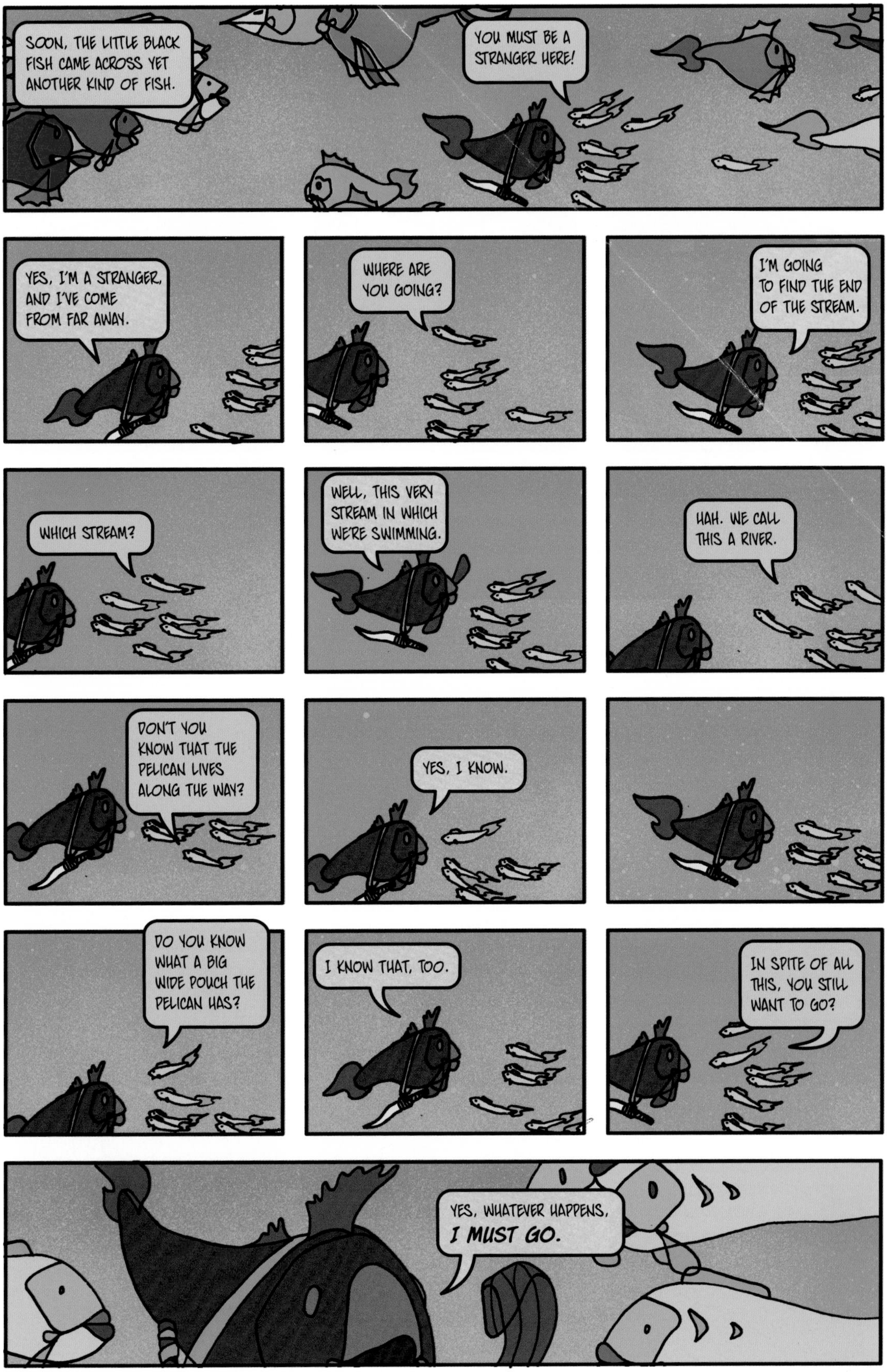
SOON, THE LITTLE BLACK FISH CAME ACROSS YET ANOTHER KIND OF FISH.
YOU MUST BE A STRANGER HERE!
YES, I'M A STRANGER, AND I'VE COME FROM FAR AWAY.
WHERE ARE YOU GOING?
I'M GOING TO FIND THE END OF THE STREAM.
WHICH STREAM?
WELL, THIS VERY STREAM IN WHICH WE'RE SWIMMING.
HAH. WE CALL THIS A RIVER.
DON'T YOU KNOW THAT THE PELICAN LIVES ALONG THE WAY?
YES, I KNOW.
DO YOU KNOW WHAT A BIG WIDE POUCH THE PELICAN HAS?
I KNOW THAT, TOO.
IN SPITE OF ALL THIS, YOU STILL WANT TO GO?
YES, WHATEVER HAPPENS, **I MUST GO.**

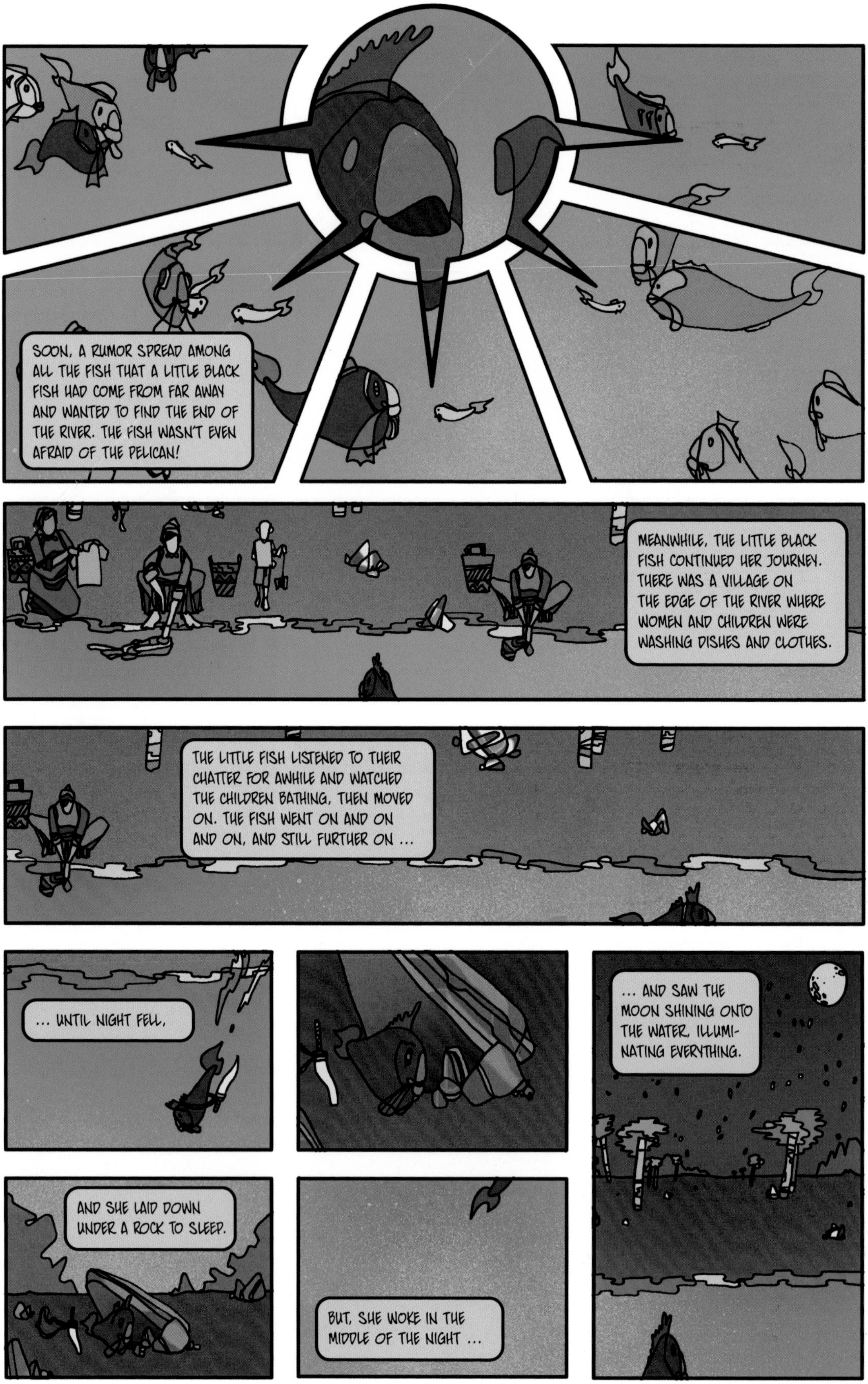
SOON, A RUMOR SPREAD AMONG ALL THE FISH THAT A LITTLE BLACK FISH HAD COME FROM FAR AWAY AND WANTED TO FIND THE END OF THE RIVER. THE FISH WASN'T EVEN AFRAID OF THE PELICAN!
MEANWHILE, THE LITTLE BLACK FISH CONTINUED HER JOURNEY. THERE WAS A VILLAGE ON THE EDGE OF THE RIVER WHERE WOMEN AND CHILDREN WERE WASHING DISHES AND CLOTHES.
THE LITTLE FISH LISTENED TO THEIR CHATTER FOR AWHILE AND WATCHED THE CHILDREN BATHING, THEN MOVED ON. THE FISH WENT ON AND ON AND ON, AND STILL FURTHER ON ...
... UNTIL NIGHT FELL,
... AND SAW THE MOON SHINING ONTO THE WATER, ILLUMINATING EVERYTHING.
AND SHE LAID DOWN UNDER A ROCK TO SLEEP.
BUT, SHE WOKE IN THE MIDDLE OF THE NIGHT ...

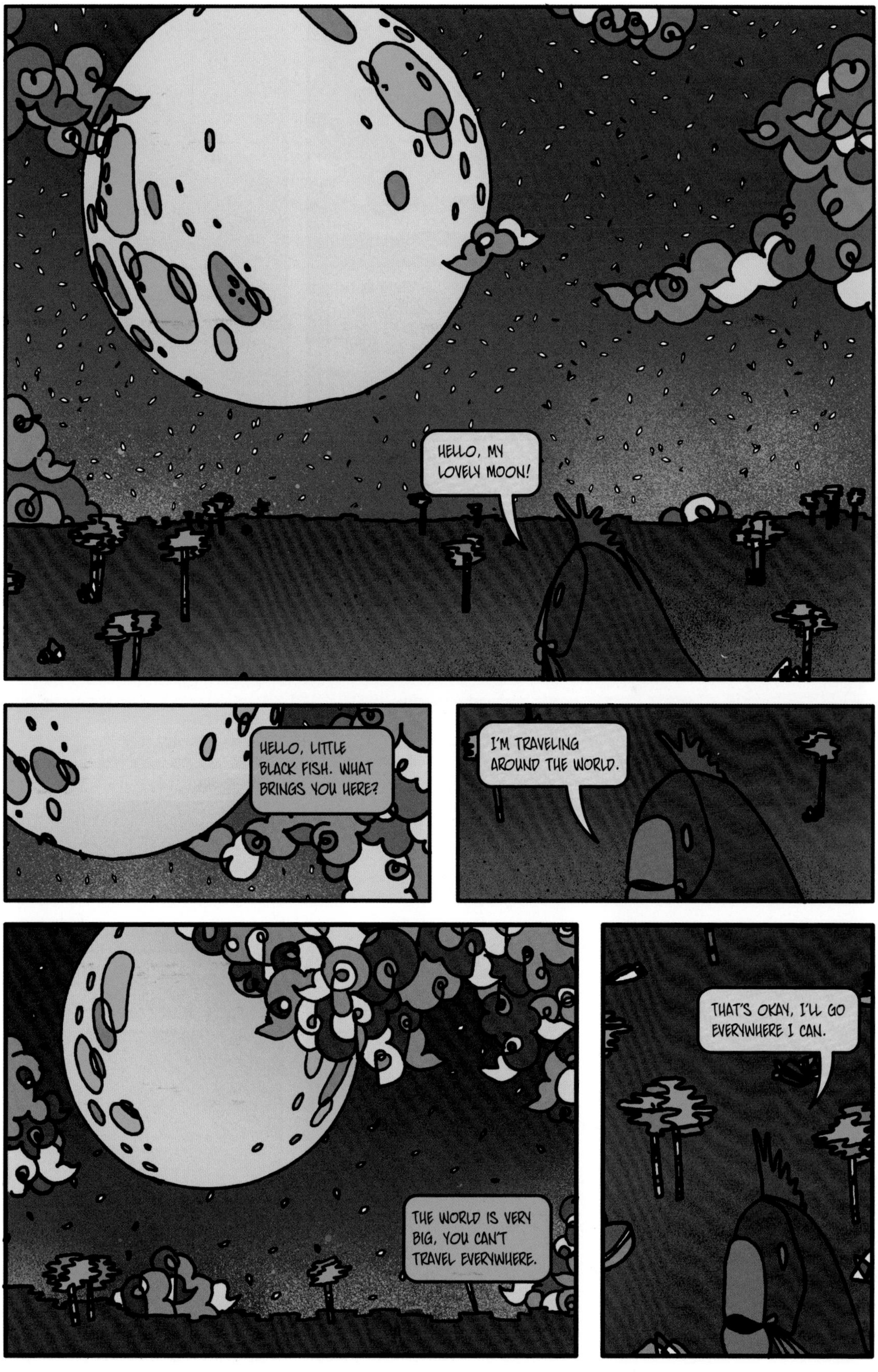
HELLO, MY LOVELY MOON!
HELLO, LITTLE BLACK FISH. WHAT BRINGS YOU HERE?
I'M TRAVELING AROUND THE WORLD.
THE WORLD IS VERY BIG, YOU CAN'T TRAVEL EVERYWHERE.
THAT'S OKAY, I'LL GO EVERYWHERE I CAN.

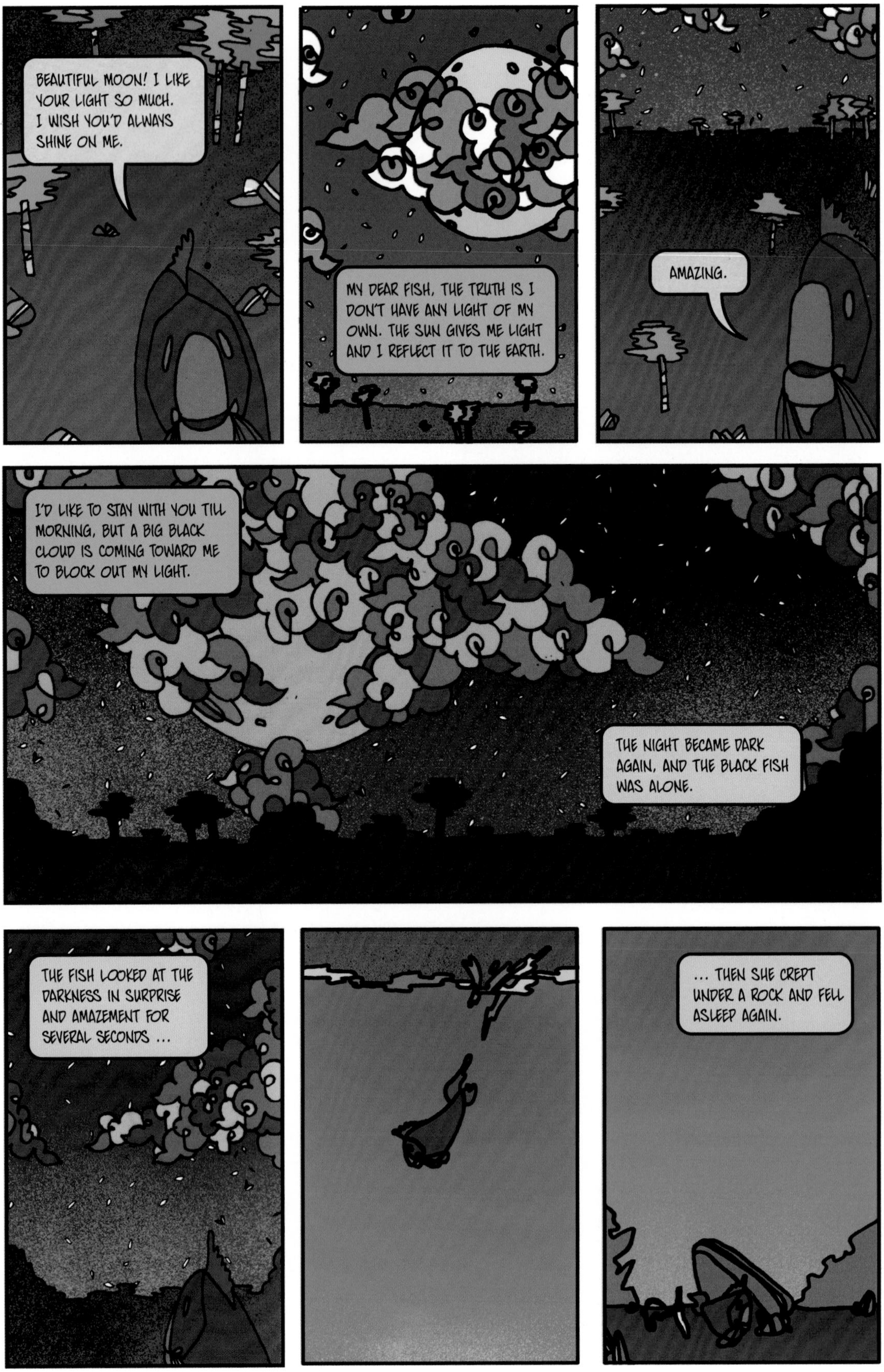
BEAUTIFUL MOON! I LIKE YOUR LIGHT SO MUCH. I WISH YOU'D ALWAYS SHINE ON ME.
MY DEAR FISH, THE TRUTH IS I DON'T HAVE ANY LIGHT OF MY OWN. THE SUN GIVES ME LIGHT AND I REFLECT IT TO THE EARTH.
AMAZING.
I'D LIKE TO STAY WITH YOU TILL MORNING, BUT A BIG BLACK CLOUD IS COMING TOWARD ME TO BLOCK OUT MY LIGHT.
THE NIGHT BECAME DARK AGAIN, AND THE BLACK FISH WAS ALONE.
THE FISH LOOKED AT THE DARKNESS IN SURPRISE AND AMAZEMENT FOR SEVERAL SECONDS ...
... THEN SHE CREPT UNDER A ROCK AND FELL ASLEEP AGAIN.

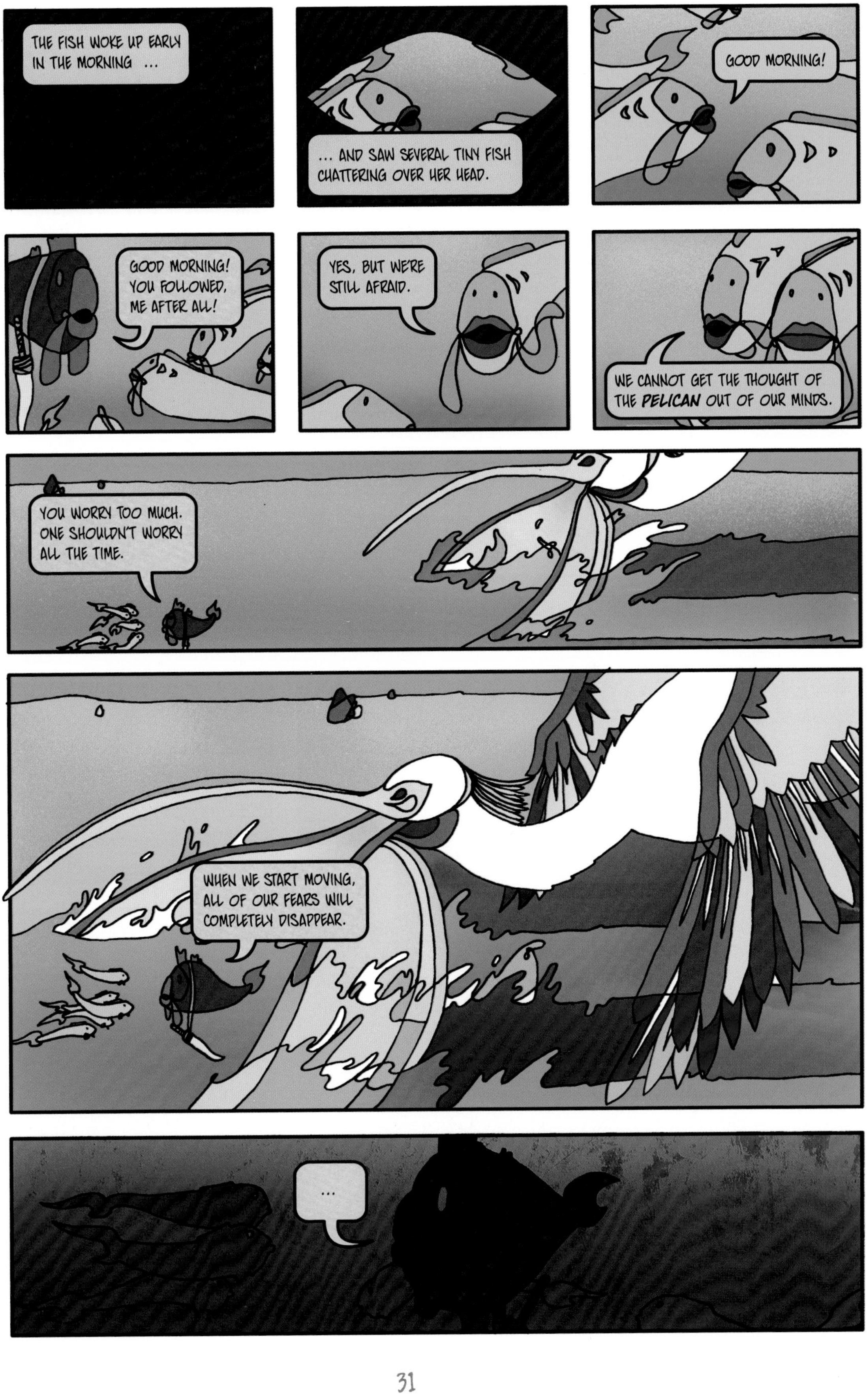
THE FISH WOKE UP EARLY IN THE MORNING ...
... AND SAW SEVERAL TINY FISH CHATTERING OVER HER HEAD.
GOOD MORNING!
GOOD MORNING! YOU FOLLOWED, ME AFTER ALL!
YES, BUT WE'RE STILL AFRAID.
WE CANNOT GET THE THOUGHT OF THE PELICAN OUT OF OUR MINDS.
YOU WORRY TOO MUCH. ONE SHOULDN'T WORRY ALL THE TIME.
WHEN WE START MOVING, ALL OF OUR FEARS WILL COMPLETELY DISAPPEAR.
...

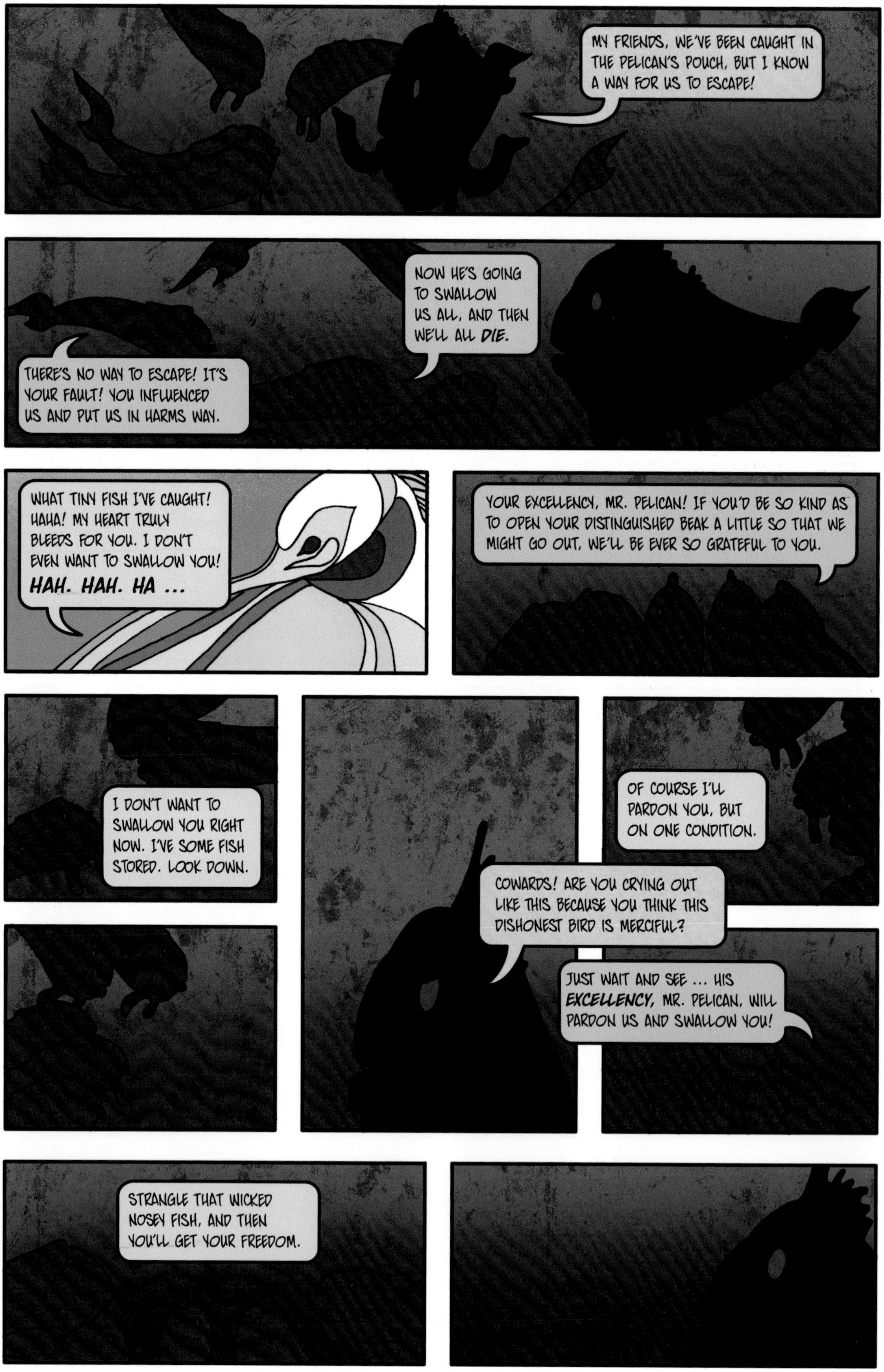
MY FRIENDS, WE'VE BEEN CAUGHT IN THE PELICAN'S POUCH, BUT I KNOW A WAY FOR US TO ESCAPE!
NOW HE'S GOING TO SWALLOW US ALL, AND THEN WE'LL ALL DIE.
THERE'S NO WAY TO ESCAPE! IT'S YOUR FAULT! YOU INFLUENCED US AND PUT US IN HARMS WAY.
WHAT TINY FISH I'VE CAUGHT! HAHA! MY HEART TRULY BLEEDS FOR YOU. I DON'T EVEN WANT TO SWALLOW YOU! HAH. HAH. HA ...
YOUR EXCELLENCY, MR. PELICAN! IF YOU'D BE SO KIND AS TO OPEN YOUR DISTINGUISHED BEAK A LITTLE SO THAT WE MIGHT GO OUT, WE'LL BE EVER SO GRATEFUL TO YOU.
I DON'T WANT TO SWALLOW YOU RIGHT NOW. I'VE SOME FISH STORED. LOOK DOWN.
COWARDS! ARE YOU CRYING OUT LIKE THIS BECAUSE YOU THINK THIS DISHONEST BIRD IS MERCIFUL?
JUST WAIT AND SEE ... HIS EXCELLENCY, MR. PELICAN, WILL PARDON US AND SWALLOW YOU!
OF COURSE I'LL PARDON YOU, BUT ON ONE CONDITION.
STRANGLE THAT WICKED NOSEY FISH, AND THEN YOU'LL GET YOUR FREEDOM.

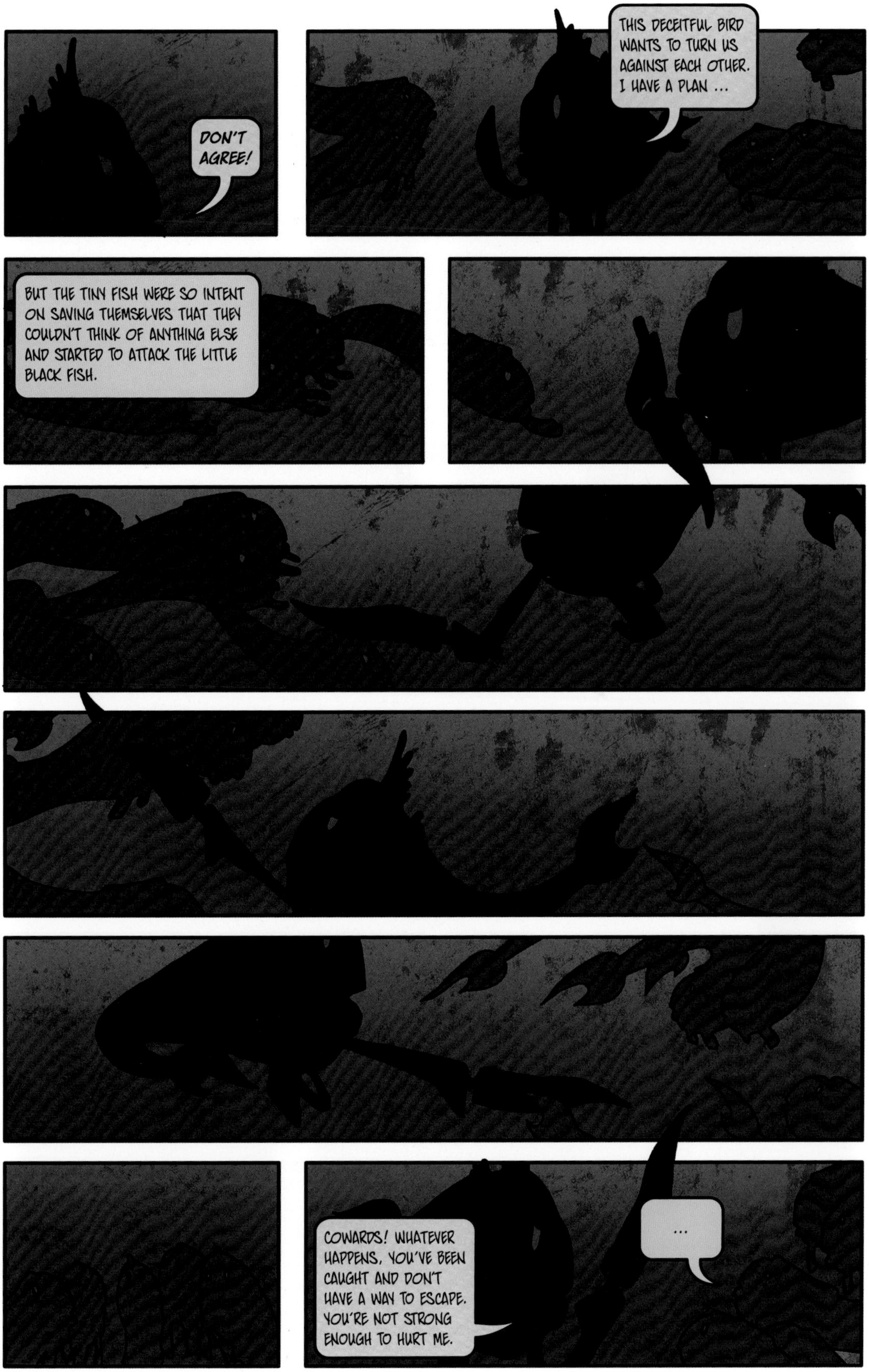
DON'T AGREE!
THIS DECEITFUL BIRD WANTS TO TURN US AGAINST EACH OTHER. I HAVE A PLAN ...
BUT THE TINY FISH WERE SO INTENT ON SAVING THEMSELVES THAT THEY COULDN'T THINK OF ANYTHING ELSE AND STARTED TO ATTACK THE LITTLE BLACK FISH.
COWARDS! WHATEVER HAPPENS, YOU'VE BEEN CAUGHT AND DON'T HAVE A WAY TO ESCAPE. YOU'RE NOT STRONG ENOUGH TO HURT ME.
...

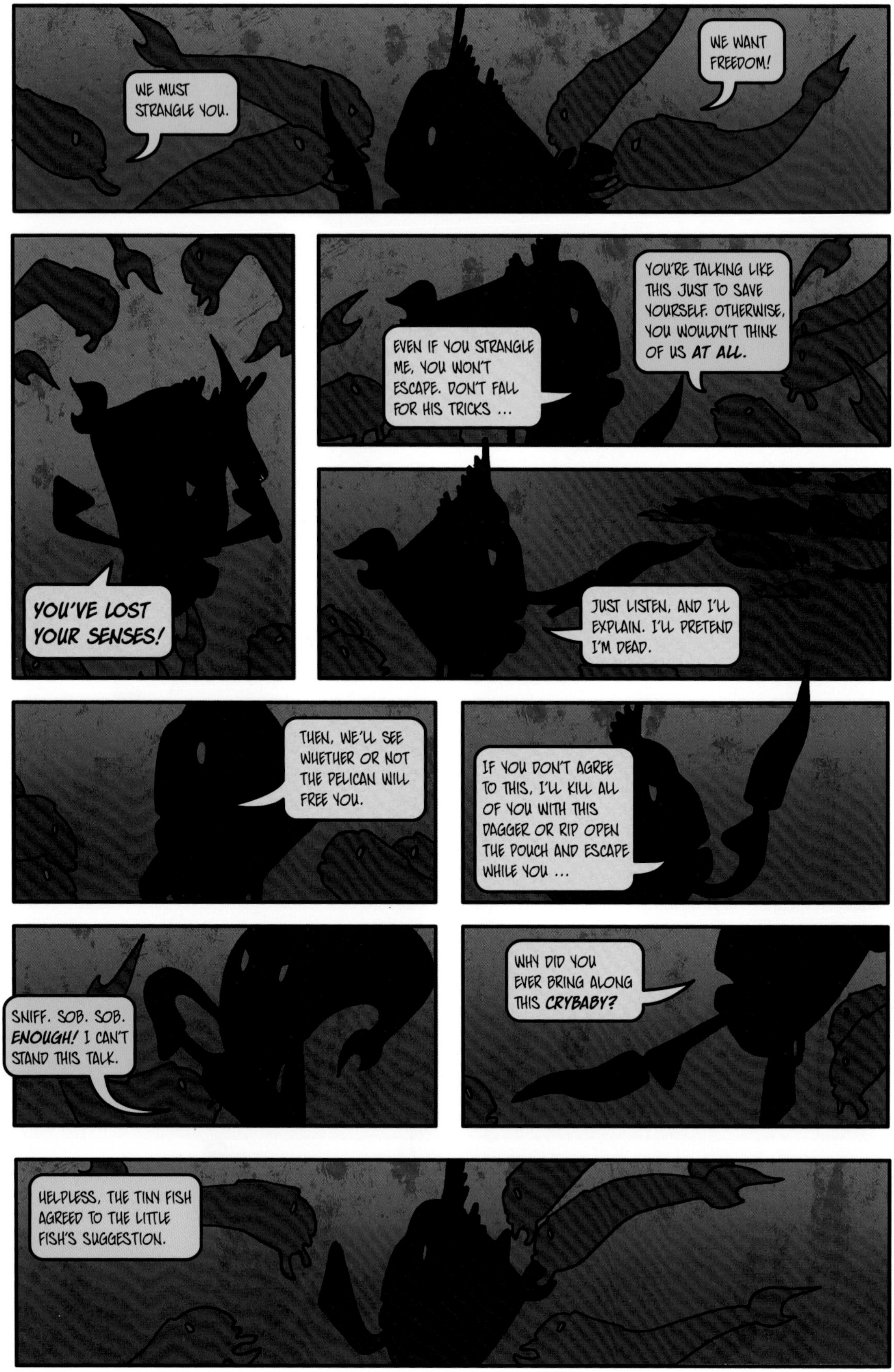
WE MUST STRANGLE YOU.
WE WANT FREEDOM!
YOU'VE LOST YOUR SENSES!
EVEN IF YOU STRANGLE ME, YOU WON'T ESCAPE. DON'T FALL FOR HIS TRICKS ...
YOU'RE TALKING LIKE THIS JUST TO SAVE YOURSELF. OTHERWISE, YOU WOULDN'T THINK OF US AT ALL.
JUST LISTEN, AND I'LL EXPLAIN. I'LL PRETEND I'M DEAD.
THEN, WE'LL SEE WHETHER OR NOT THE PELICAN WILL FREE YOU.
IF YOU DON'T AGREE TO THIS, I'LL KILL ALL OF YOU WITH THIS DAGGER OR RIP OPEN THE POUCH AND ESCAPE WHILE YOU ...
SNIFF. SOB. SOB. ENOUGH! I CAN'T STAND THIS TALK.
WHY DID YOU EVER BRING ALONG THIS CRYBABY?
HELPLESS, THE TINY FISH AGREED TO THE LITTLE FISH'S SUGGESTION.

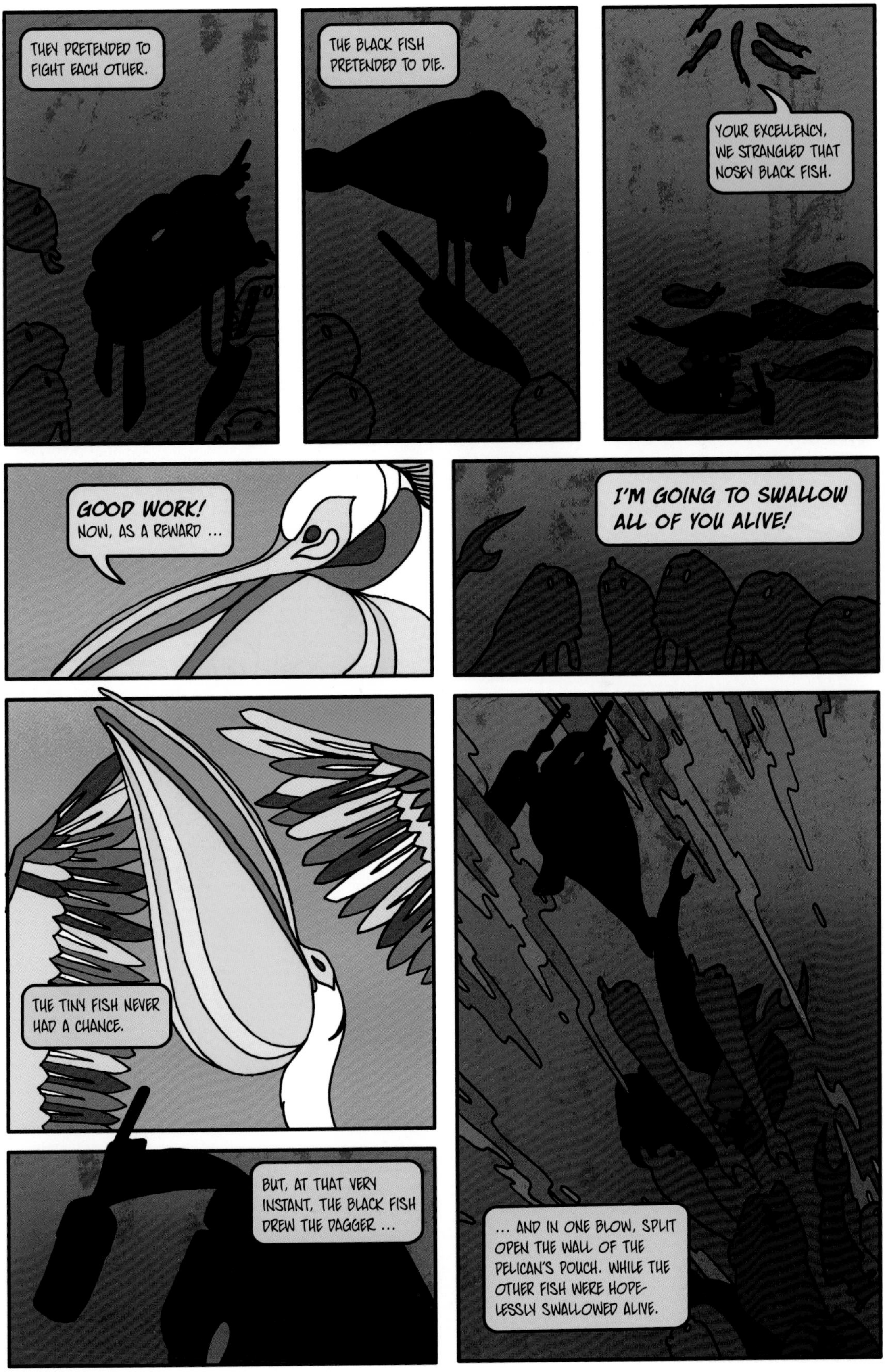
THEY PRETENDED TO FIGHT EACH OTHER.
THE BLACK FISH PRETENDED TO DIE.
YOUR EXCELLENCY, WE STRANGLED THAT NOSEY BLACK FISH.
GOOD WORK! NOW, AS A REWARD ...
I'M GOING TO SWALLOW ALL OF YOU ALIVE!
THE TINY FISH NEVER HAD A CHANCE.
BUT, AT THAT VERY INSTANT, THE BLACK FISH DREW THE DAGGER ...
... AND IN ONE BLOW, SPLIT OPEN THE WALL OF THE PELICAN'S POUCH. WHILE THE OTHER FISH WERE HOPE-LESSLY SWALLOWED ALIVE.

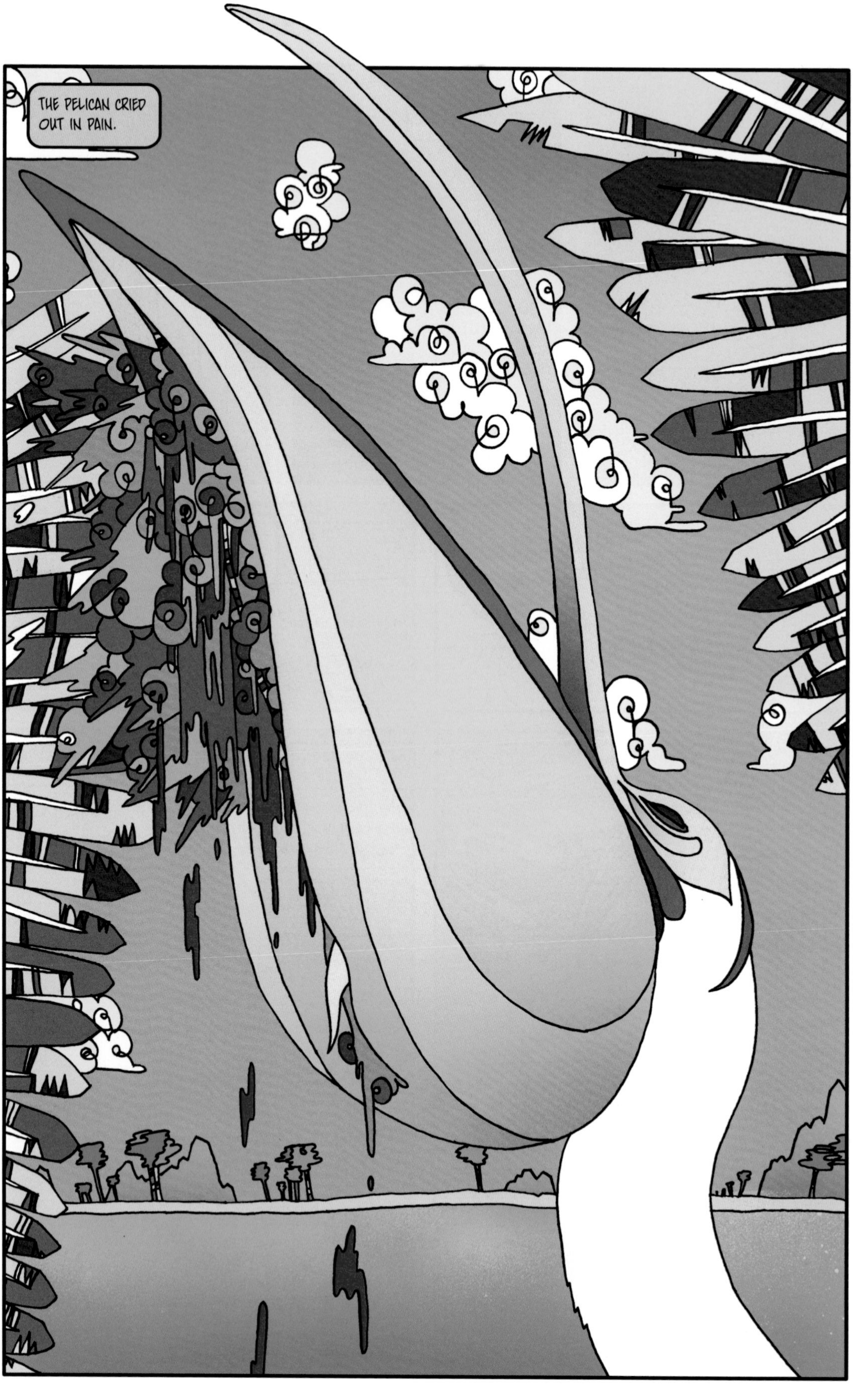
THE PELICAN CRIED OUT IN PAIN.

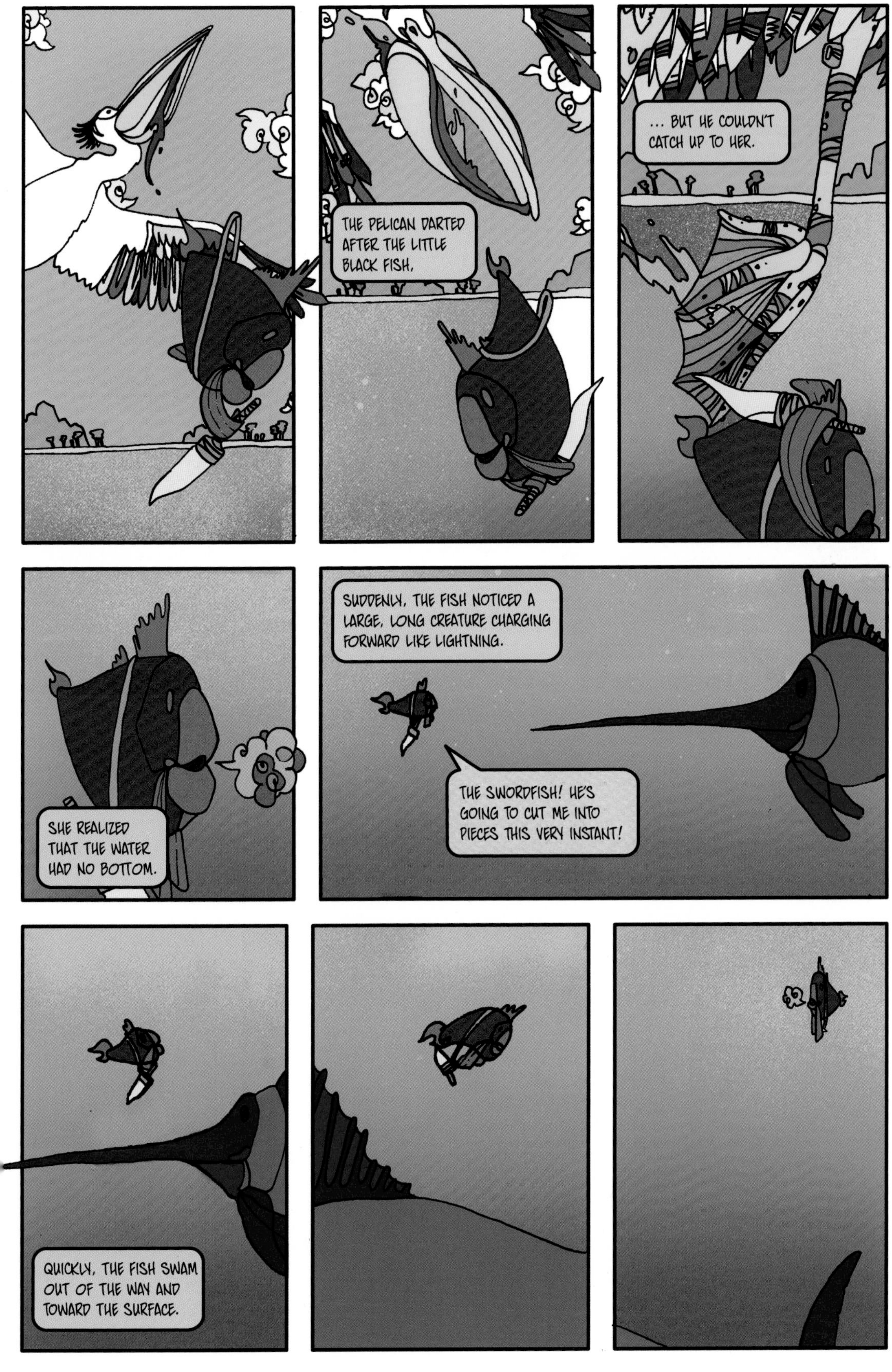
THE PELICAN DARTED AFTER THE LITTLE BLACK FISH,
... BUT HE COULDN'T CATCH UP TO HER.
SHE REALIZED THAT THE WATER HAD NO BOTTOM.
SUDDENLY, THE FISH NOTICED A LARGE, LONG CREATURE CHARGING FORWARD LIKE LIGHTNING.
THE SWORDFISH! HE'S GOING TO CUT ME INTO PIECES THIS VERY INSTANT!
QUICKLY, THE FISH SWAM OUT OF THE WAY AND TOWARD THE SURFACE.

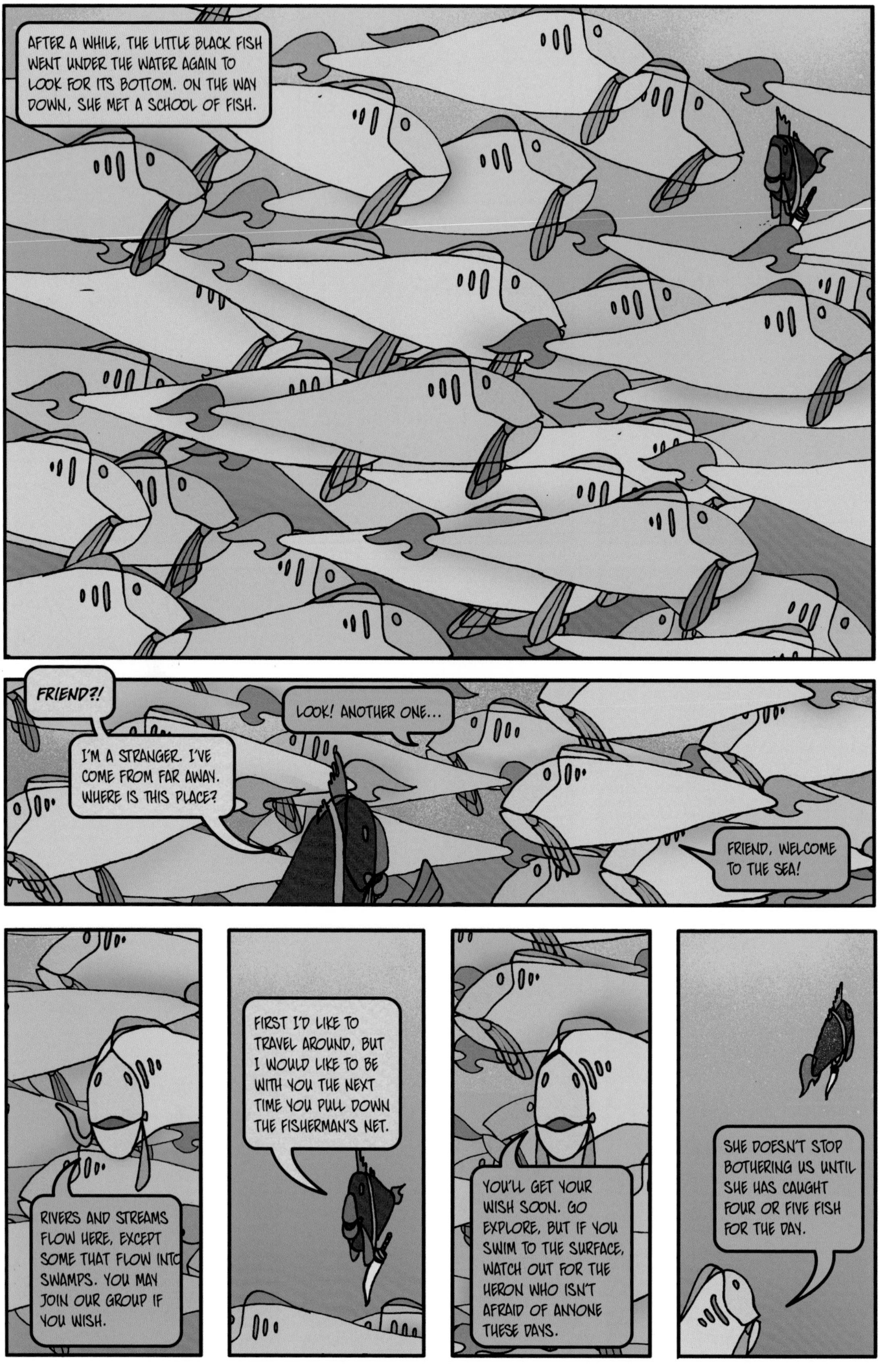

AFTER A WHILE, THE LITTLE BLACK FISH WENT UNDER THE WATER AGAIN TO LOOK FOR ITS BOTTOM. ON THE WAY DOWN, SHE MET A SCHOOL OF FISH.
FRIEND?!
I'M A STRANGER. I'VE COME FROM FAR AWAY. WHERE IS THIS PLACE?
LOOK! ANOTHER ONE...
FRIEND, WELCOME TO THE SEA!
RIVERS AND STREAMS FLOW HERE, EXCEPT SOME THAT FLOW INTO SWAMPS. YOU MAY JOIN OUR GROUP IF YOU WISH.
FIRST I'D LIKE TO TRAVEL AROUND, BUT I WOULD LIKE TO BE WITH YOU THE NEXT TIME YOU PULL DOWN THE FISHERMAN'S NET.
YOU'LL GET YOUR WISH SOON. GO EXPLORE, BUT IF YOU SWIM TO THE SURFACE, WATCH OUT FOR THE HERON WHO ISN'T AFRAID OF ANYONE THESE DAYS.
SHE DOESN'T STOP BOTHERING US UNTIL SHE HAS CAUGHT FOUR OR FIVE FISH FOR THE DAY.

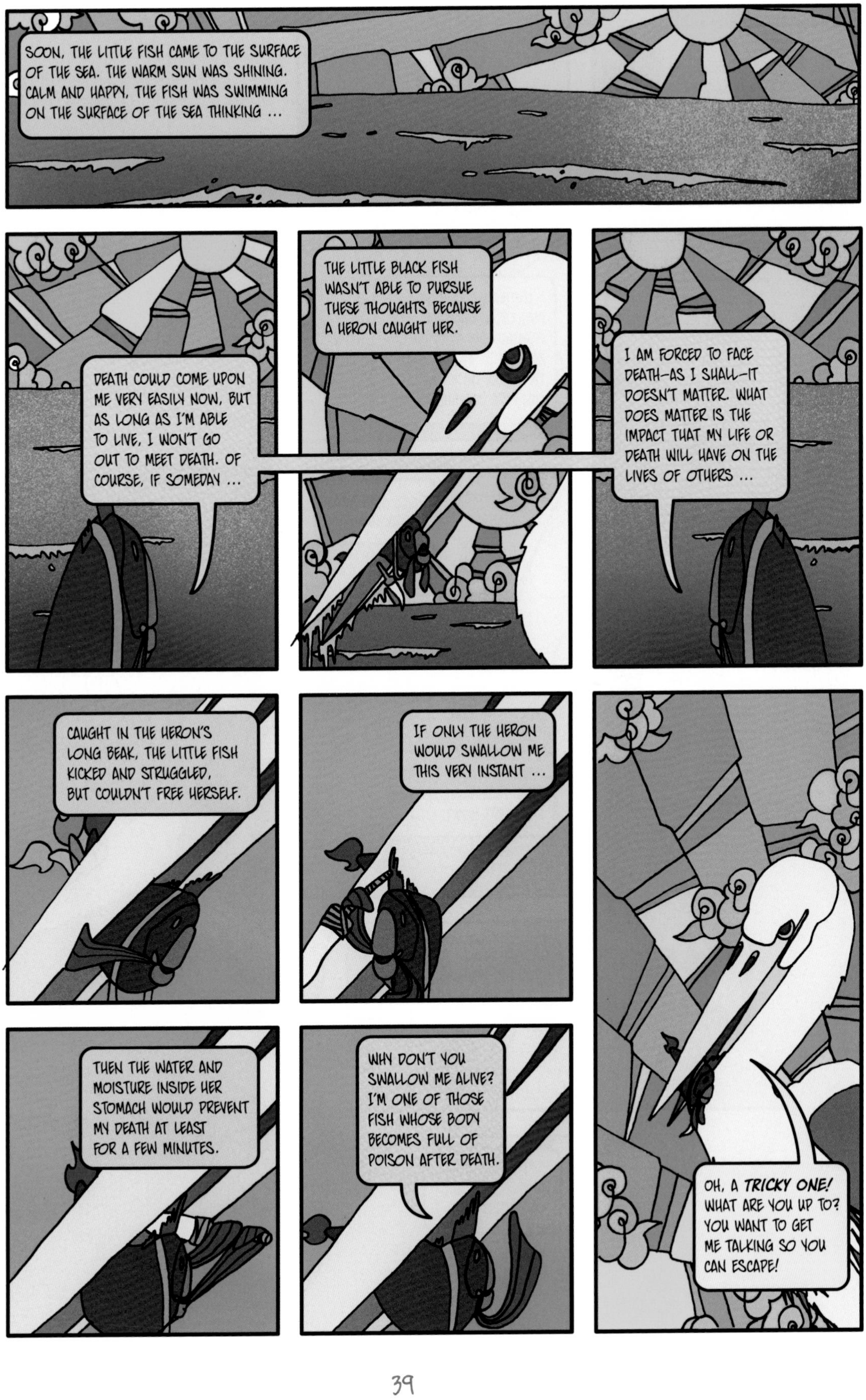
SOON, THE LITTLE FISH CAME TO THE SURFACE OF THE SEA. THE WARM SUN WAS SHINING. CALM AND HAPPY, THE FISH WAS SWIMMING ON THE SURFACE OF THE SEA THINKING ...
DEATH COULD COME UPON ME VERY EASILY NOW, BUT AS LONG AS I'M ABLE TO LIVE, I WON'T GO OUT TO MEET DEATH. OF COURSE, IF SOMEDAY ...
THE LITTLE BLACK FISH WASN'T ABLE TO PURSUE THESE THOUGHTS BECAUSE A HERON CAUGHT HER.
I AM FORCED TO FACE DEATH—AS I SHALL—IT DOESN'T MATTER. WHAT DOES MATTER IS THE IMPACT THAT MY LIFE OR DEATH WILL HAVE ON THE LIVES OF OTHERS ...
CAUGHT IN THE HERON'S LONG BEAK, THE LITTLE FISH KICKED AND STRUGGLED, BUT COULDN'T FREE HERSELF.
IF ONLY THE HERON WOULD SWALLOW ME THIS VERY INSTANT ...
THEN THE WATER AND MOISTURE INSIDE HER STOMACH WOULD PREVENT MY DEATH AT LEAST FOR A FEW MINUTES.
WHY DON'T YOU SWALLOW ME ALIVE? I'M ONE OF THOSE FISH WHOSE BODY BECOMES FULL OF POISON AFTER DEATH.
OH, A ***TRICKY ONE!*** WHAT ARE YOU UP TO? YOU WANT TO GET ME TALKING SO YOU CAN ESCAPE!

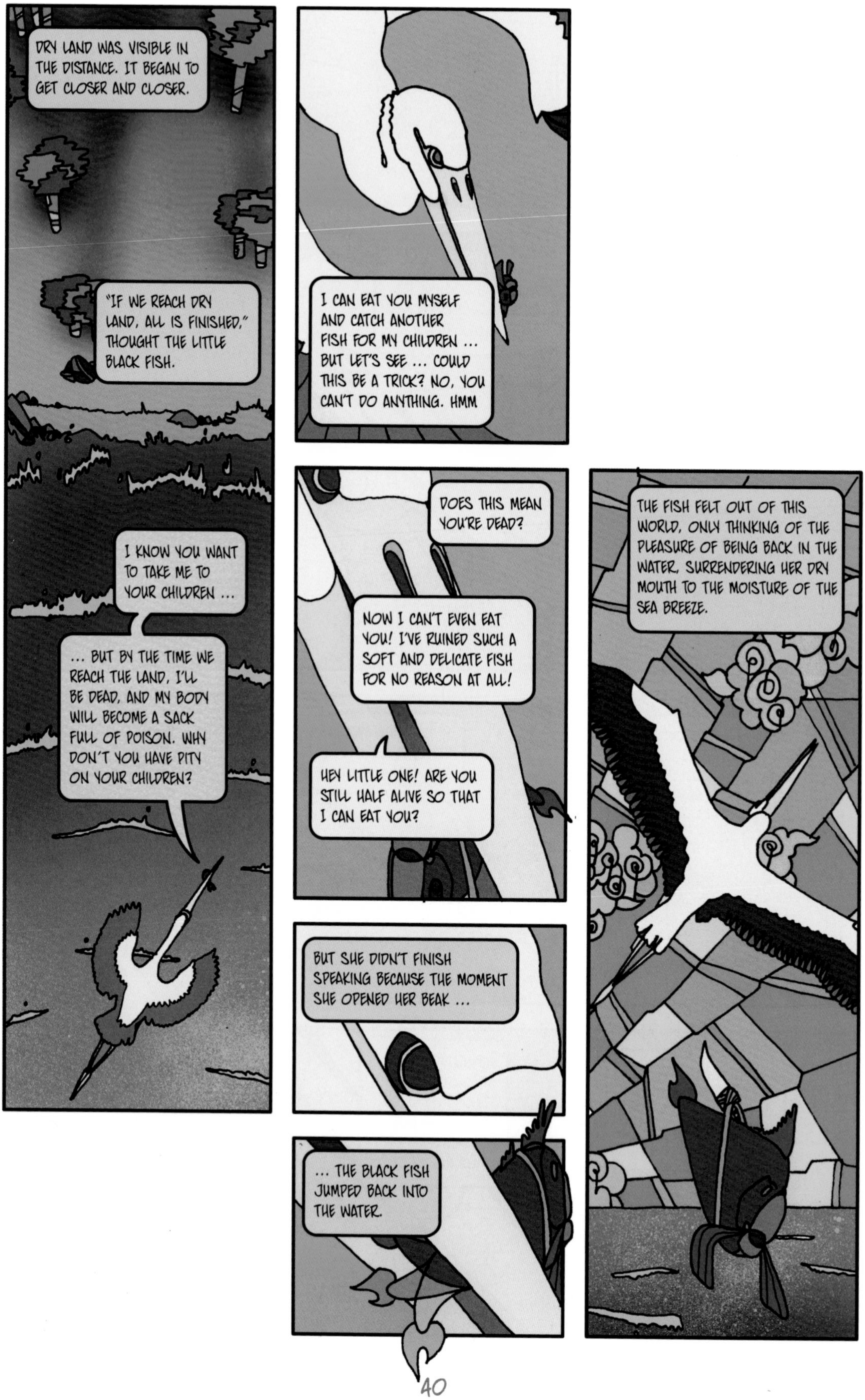
DRY LAND WAS VISIBLE IN THE DISTANCE. IT BEGAN TO GET CLOSER AND CLOSER.
"IF WE REACH DRY LAND, ALL IS FINISHED," THOUGHT THE LITTLE BLACK FISH.
I KNOW YOU WANT TO TAKE ME TO YOUR CHILDREN ...
... BUT BY THE TIME WE REACH THE LAND, I'LL BE DEAD, AND MY BODY WILL BECOME A SACK FULL OF POISON. WHY DON'T YOU HAVE PITY ON YOUR CHILDREN?
I CAN EAT YOU MYSELF AND CATCH ANOTHER FISH FOR MY CHILDREN ... BUT LET'S SEE ... COULD THIS BE A TRICK? NO, YOU CAN'T DO ANYTHING. HMM
DOES THIS MEAN YOU'RE DEAD?
NOW I CAN'T EVEN EAT YOU! I'VE RUINED SUCH A SOFT AND DELICATE FISH FOR NO REASON AT ALL!
HEY LITTLE ONE! ARE YOU STILL HALF ALIVE SO THAT I CAN EAT YOU?
BUT SHE DIDN'T FINISH SPEAKING BECAUSE THE MOMENT SHE OPENED HER BEAK ...
... THE BLACK FISH JUMPED BACK INTO THE WATER.
THE FISH FELT OUT OF THIS WORLD, ONLY THINKING OF THE PLEASURE OF BEING BACK IN THE WATER, SURRENDERING HER DRY MOUTH TO THE MOISTURE OF THE SEA BREEZE.

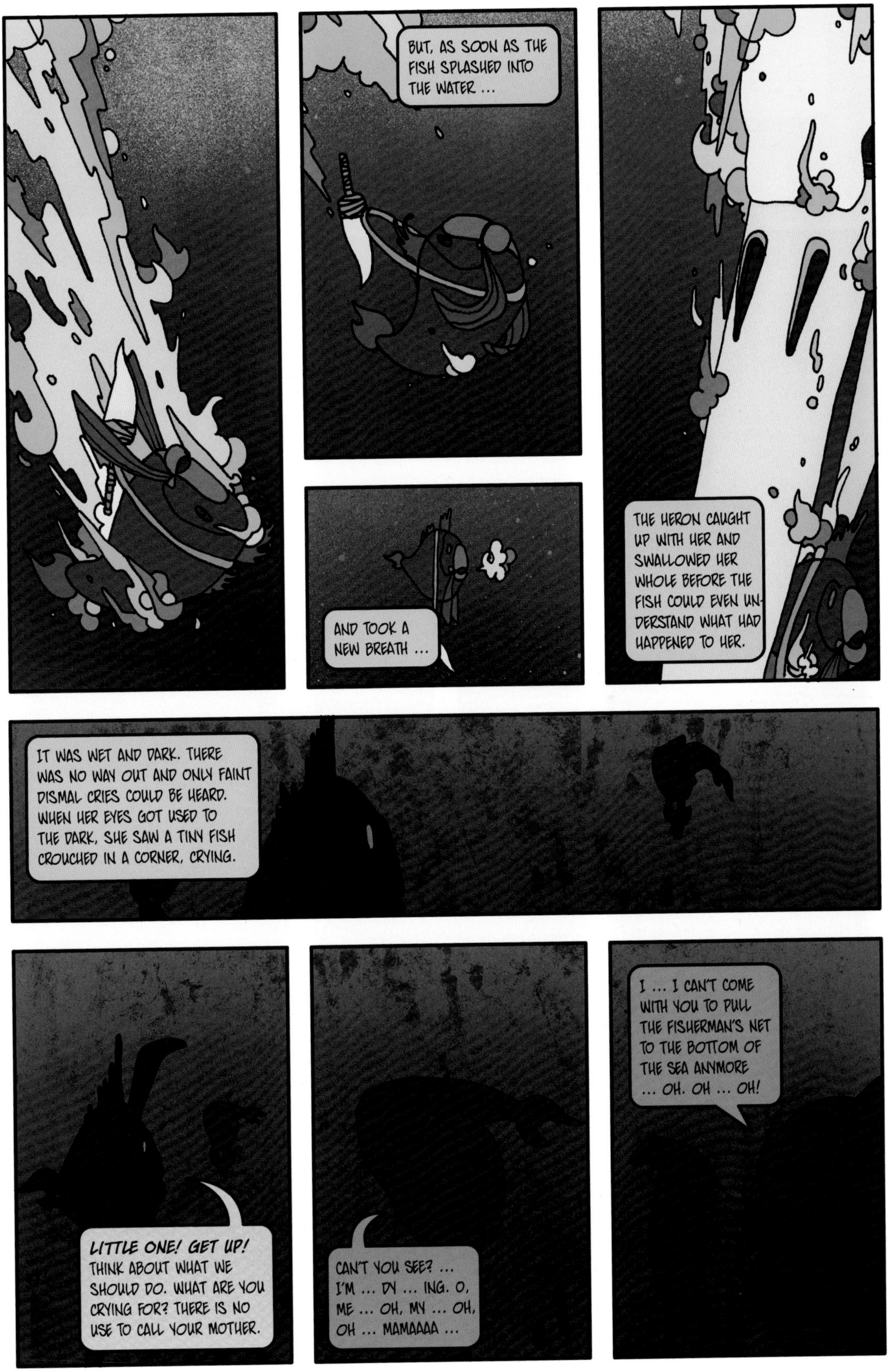

BUT, AS SOON AS THE FISH SPLASHED INTO THE WATER ...
AND TOOK A NEW BREATH ...
THE HERON CAUGHT UP WITH HER AND SWALLOWED HER WHOLE BEFORE THE FISH COULD EVEN UNDERSTAND WHAT HAD HAPPENED TO HER.
IT WAS WET AND DARK. THERE WAS NO WAY OUT AND ONLY FAINT DISMAL CRIES COULD BE HEARD. WHEN HER EYES GOT USED TO THE DARK, SHE SAW A TINY FISH CROUCHED IN A CORNER, CRYING.
LITTLE ONE! GET UP! THINK ABOUT WHAT WE SHOULD DO. WHAT ARE YOU CRYING FOR? THERE IS NO USE TO CALL YOUR MOTHER.
CAN'T YOU SEE? ... I'M ... DY ... ING. O, ME ... OH, MY ... OH, OH ... MAMAAAA ...
I ... I CAN'T COME WITH YOU TO PULL THE FISHERMAN'S NET TO THE BOTTOM OF THE SEA ANYMORE ... OH. OH ... OH!

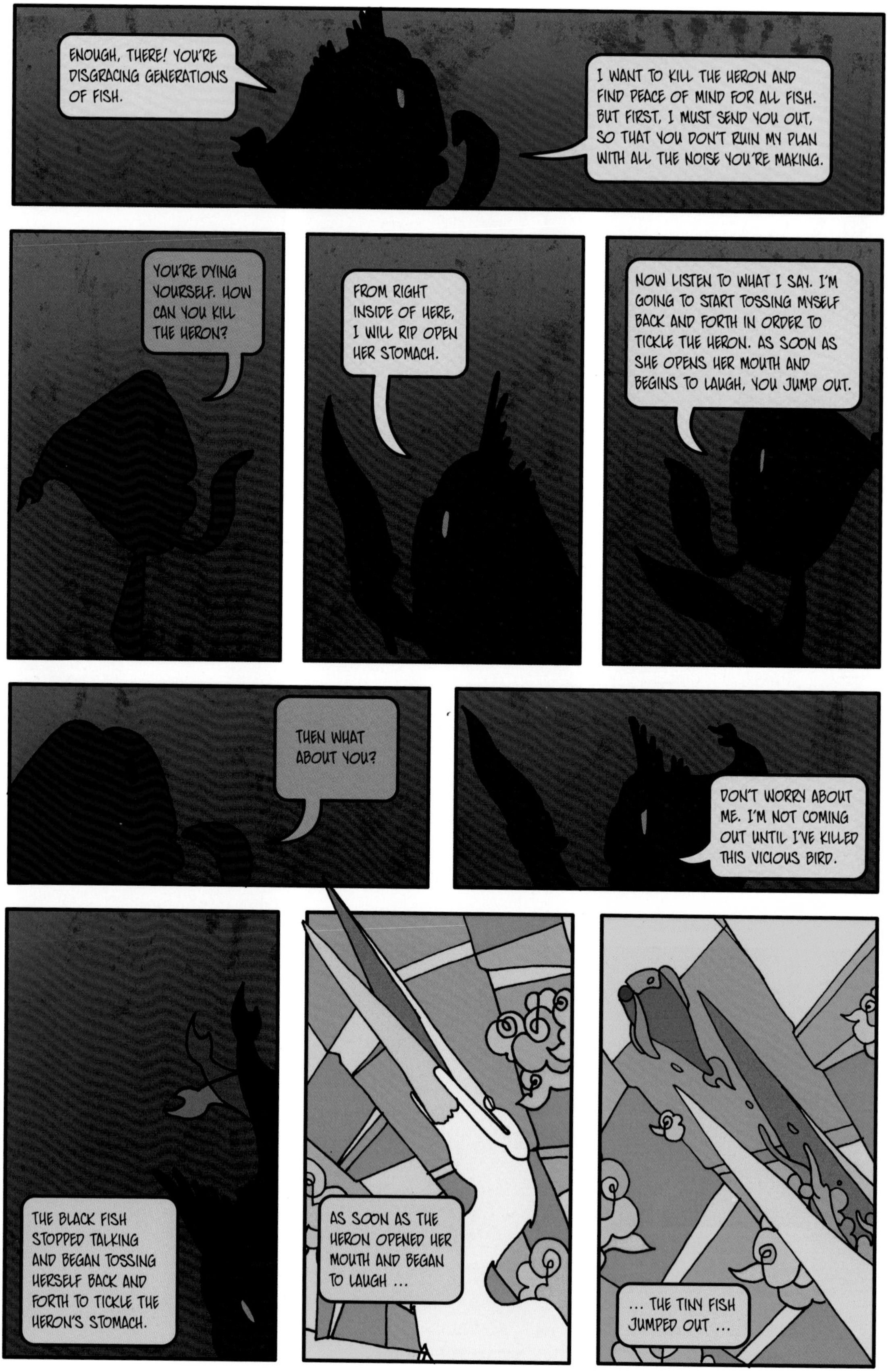
ENOUGH, THERE! YOU'RE DISGRACING GENERATIONS OF FISH.
I WANT TO KILL THE HERON AND FIND PEACE OF MIND FOR ALL FISH. BUT FIRST, I MUST SEND YOU OUT, SO THAT YOU DON'T RUIN MY PLAN WITH ALL THE NOISE YOU'RE MAKING.
YOU'RE DYING YOURSELF. HOW CAN YOU KILL THE HERON?
FROM RIGHT INSIDE OF HERE, I WILL RIP OPEN HER STOMACH.
NOW LISTEN TO WHAT I SAY. I'M GOING TO START TOSSING MYSELF BACK AND FORTH IN ORDER TO TICKLE THE HERON. AS SOON AS SHE OPENS HER MOUTH AND BEGINS TO LAUGH, YOU JUMP OUT.
THEN WHAT ABOUT YOU?
DON'T WORRY ABOUT ME. I'M NOT COMING OUT UNTIL I'VE KILLED THIS VICIOUS BIRD.
THE BLACK FISH STOPPED TALKING AND BEGAN TOSSING HERSELF BACK AND FORTH TO TICKLE THE HERON'S STOMACH.
AS SOON AS THE HERON OPENED HER MOUTH AND BEGAN TO LAUGH ...
... THE TINY FISH JUMPED OUT ...

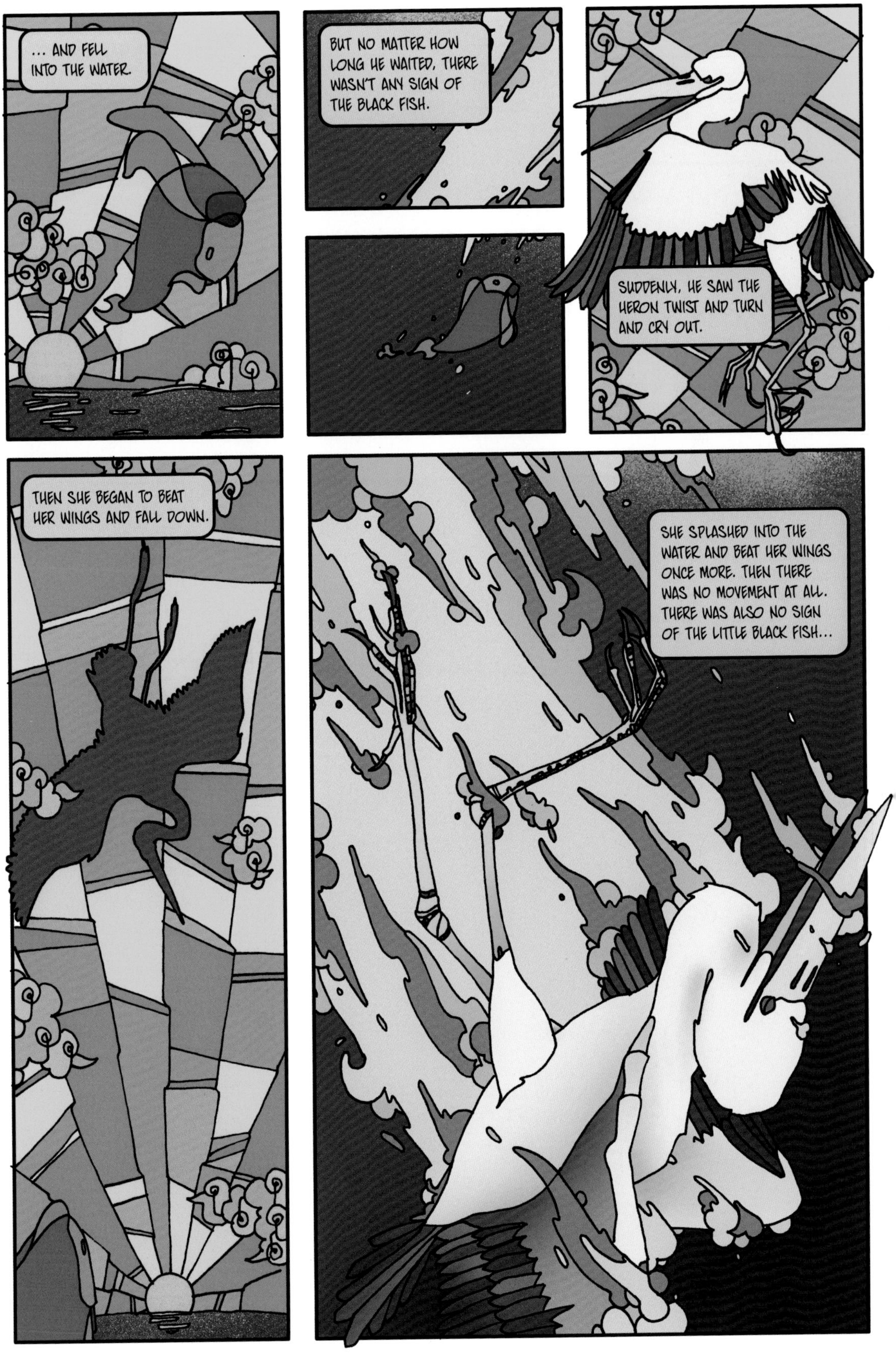
... AND FELL INTO THE WATER.
BUT NO MATTER HOW LONG HE WAITED, THERE WASN'T ANY SIGN OF THE BLACK FISH.
SUDDENLY, HE SAW THE HERON TWIST AND TURN AND CRY OUT.
THEN SHE BEGAN TO BEAT HER WINGS AND FALL DOWN.
SHE SPLASHED INTO THE WATER AND BEAT HER WINGS ONCE MORE. THEN THERE WAS NO MOVEMENT AT ALL. THERE WAS ALSO NO SIGN OF THE LITTLE BLACK FISH...

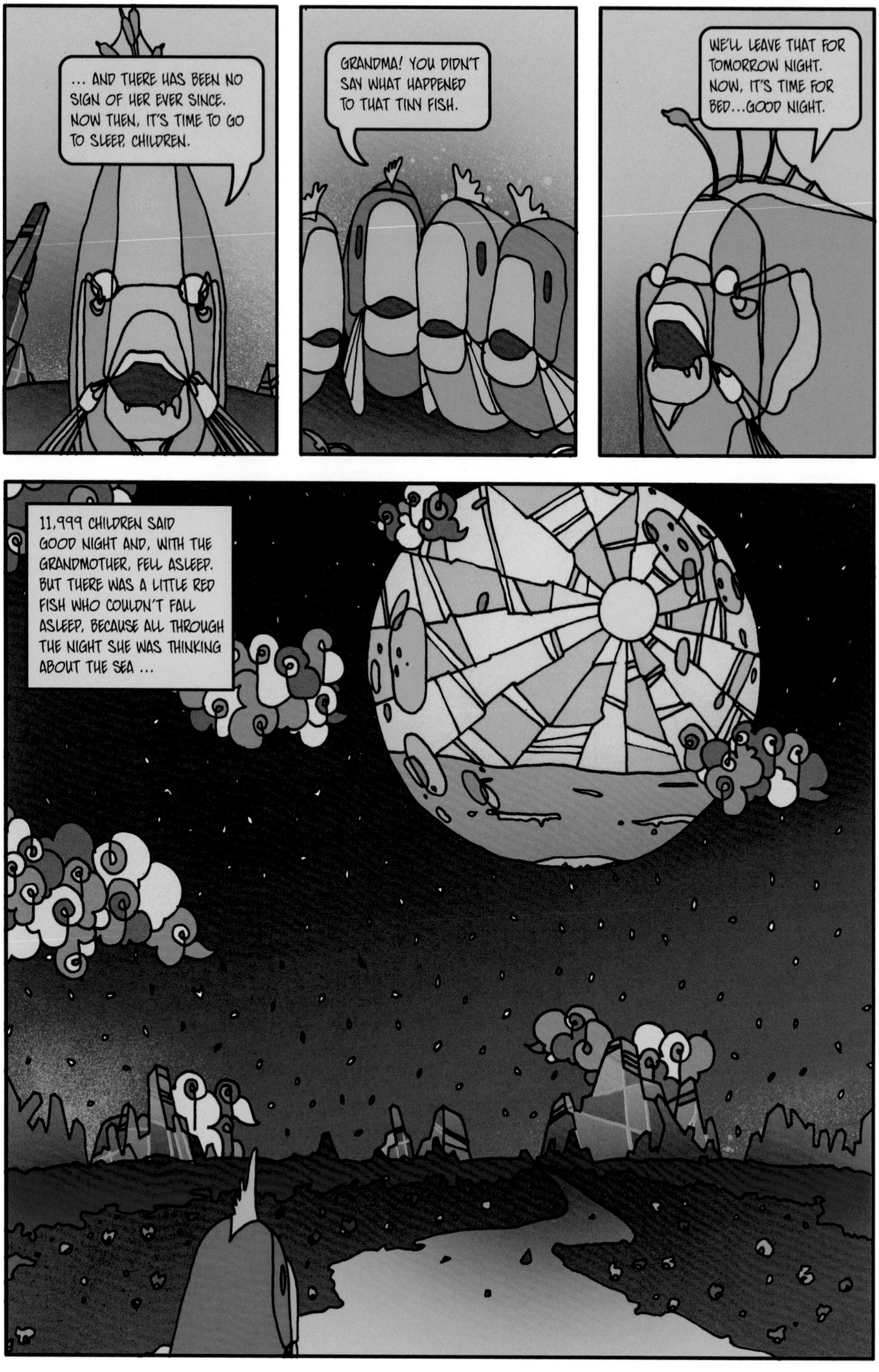
... AND THERE HAS BEEN NO SIGN OF HER EVER SINCE. NOW THEN, IT'S TIME TO GO TO SLEEP, CHILDREN.
GRANDMA! YOU DIDN'T SAY WHAT HAPPENED TO THAT TINY FISH.
WE'LL LEAVE THAT FOR TOMORROW NIGHT. NOW, IT'S TIME FOR BED...GOOD NIGHT.
11,999 CHILDREN SAID GOOD NIGHT AND, WITH THE GRANDMOTHER, FELL ASLEEP. BUT THERE WAS A LITTLE RED FISH WHO COULDN'T FALL ASLEEP, BECAUSE ALL THROUGH THE NIGHT SHE WAS THINKING ABOUT THE SEA ...

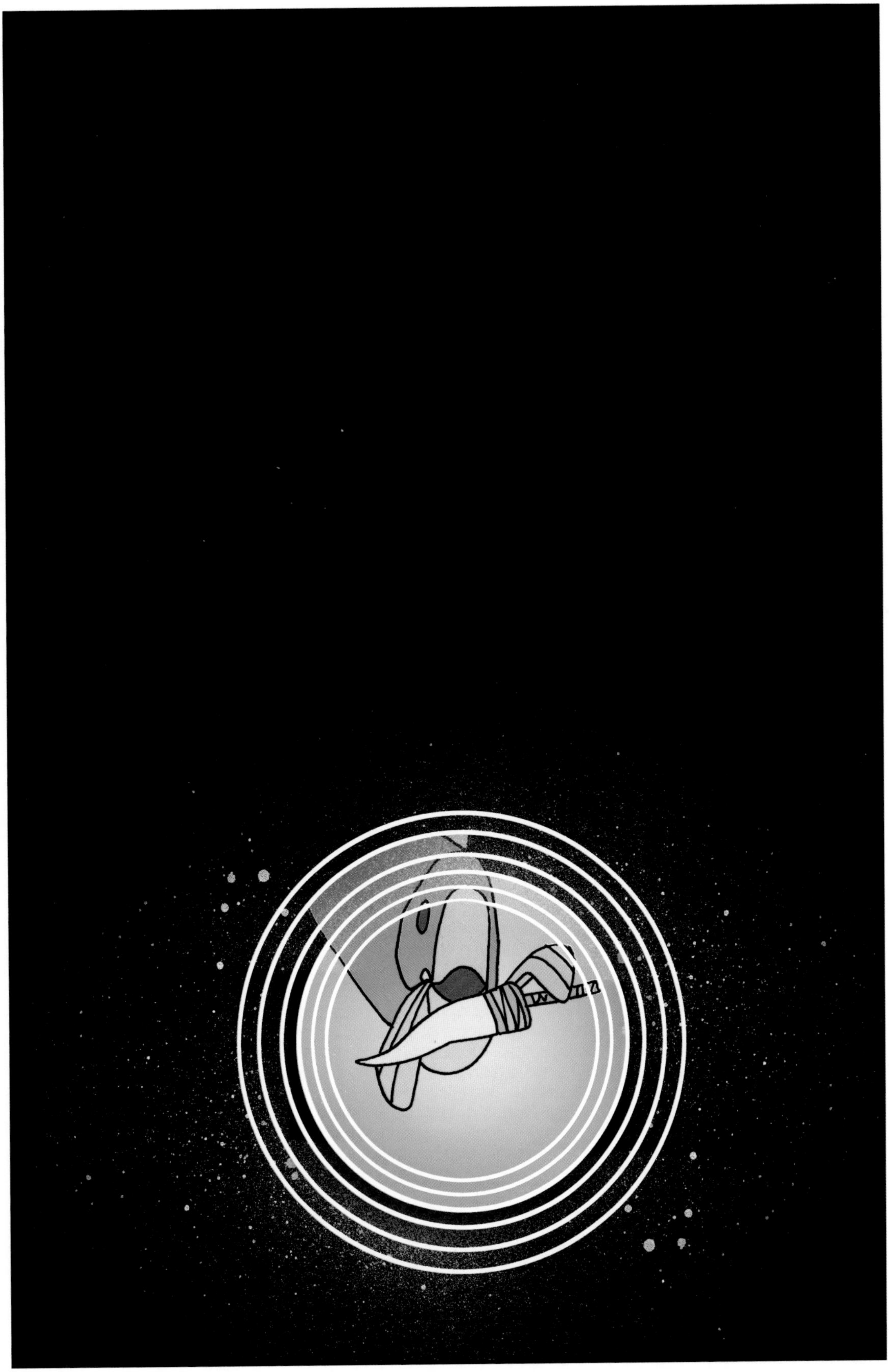

AFTERWORD
BY BIZHAN KHODABANDEH

AFTER ENDLESS HOURS OF STUDYING TEXTS ON COMICS
BY SCOTT McCLOUD AND WILL EISNER, I FINALLY BUILT
UP ENOUGH CONFIDENCE TO START MY FIRST COMIC, THIS
ADAPTATION OF *"THE LITTLE BLACK FISH."*

I CHOSE THIS STORY BECAUSE ITS MORALS TRANSCEND
THE BOUNDARIES OF ANY SPECIFIC POLITICAL IDEOLOGY.
IT IS ABOUT QUESTIONING AUTHORITY, SELF-SACRIFICE,
AND LEAVING A LEGACY FOR THE NEXT GENERATION.
THESE LESSONS ARE IMPORTANT FOR OUR CHILDREN
AND ARE MORALS OF WHICH ADULTS NEED TO BE
FREQUENTLY REMINDED.

AS FOR MY ADAPTATION, I MADE A COUPLE OF CHANGES
TO THE STORY THAT I HOPE DON'T UPSET ANYONE. THE
LIZARD ORIGINALLY FASHIONS A DAGGER OUT OF GRASS
AND THORNS. I THOUGHT THAT A HORNED LIZARD SACRIFIC-
ING ITS OWN HORN MADE MORE SENSE TO MY ADAPTATION
AND ADDED DRAMATIC EFFECT.

I ALSO OMITTED A STATEMENT MADE BY THE MOON
ABOUT THE UNITED STATES MOON LANDING. ALTHOUGH
IT DIGRESSED INTO AN IMPORTANT LESSON ABOUT THE
POTENTIAL OF HUMANS, IT SEEMED OUT OF PLACE IN THIS
VERSION OF THE STORY.

I STRUGGLED WITH THESE CHANGES FOR HOURS. I KEPT
TELLING MYSELF THAT THIS IS AN ADAPTATION, NOT A
DIRECT TRANSLATION. THE MAJORITY OF THE TEXT IS
VISUAL AND HAS ALREADY CHANGED BEHRANGI'S WORDS.
LIKE ALL STORY TELLERS, I GAVE SOME OF MYSELF
THROUGH THE PROCESS OF RETELLING HIS STORY.

I HOPE IT'S SOMETHING THAT WOULD HAVE MADE
BEHRANGHI PROUD.

THE AUTHOR

THIS BIOGRAPHY IS INCOMPLETE BECAUSE RESOURCES ON BEHRANGI ARE LIMITED. TO PROVIDE A BETTER CONTEXT FOR THE STORY, PLEASE THINK OF THIS BIOGRAPHY AS A SNAPSHOT OF BEHRANGI'S LIFE...

SAMAD BEHRANGI (1939-1968), WAS AN IRANIAN-BORN TEACHER, SOCIAL CRITIC, WRITER AND ACTIVIST. HE GREW UP IN A WORKING CLASS FAMILY NEAR TABRIZ, A CITY LOCATED IN NORTHEASTERN IRAN.

AFTER FINISHING ELEMENTARY AND SECONDARY SCHOOL, HE FELT COMPELLED TO ATTEND TEACHER TRAINING SCHOOL. IN 1957, HE SUCCESSFULLY COMPLETED HIS TRAINING AND BEGAN TO TEACH FOR WHAT WOULD END UP BEING 11 YEARS IN RURAL AZERBAJANI SCHOOLS. DURING THIS TIME HE WAS AWARDED A BACHELOR'S DEGREE IN ENGLISH THROUGH TABRIZ UNIVERSITY.

BEHRANGI WAS ESPECIALLY ENAMORED BY FOLKTALES—MORE SPECIFICALLY, AZERI FOLKTALES. HIS FASCINATION FOR THESE STORIES, AND THEIR ABILITY TO DISCUSS COMPLEX SOCIAL ISSUES, RESULTED IN "...THE PUBLICATION OF AN ESSAY ON EDUCATIONAL PROBLEMS, SEVERAL ORIGINAL CHILDREN'S STORIES DEALING REALISTICALLY WITH SOCIAL ISSUES, AND A SECOND VOLUME OF AZERI FOLKTALES THAT ESTABLISHED HIS REPUTATION AS A RISING STAR AMONG A NEW GENERATION OF WRITERS." (IRAN CHAMBER SOCIETY, 2011).

BEHRANGI'S REPUTATION AS A DISSIDENT AND HIS RELATIONSHIP TO THE LEFTIST MOVEMENT, LED SOME ACTIVISTS TO BELIEVE THAT HIS UNTIMELY DEATH WAS A POLITICAL ASSASSINATION CARRIED OUT BY THE SHAH'S SAVAK AGENTS (THE SHAH'S SECURITY AGENTS).

OTHERS BELIEVE HIS DEATH TO MERELY BE AN UNFORTUNATE EVENT.

AT THE AGE OF 29, BEHRANGI'S BODY HAD BEEN FOUND DROWNED IN THE ARAS RIVER. IT WASN'T UNTIL AFTER HIS DEATH THAT HIS MOST POPULAR BOOK, *THE LITTLE BLACK FISH*, WAS PUBLISHED.

THE STORY

THE LITTLE BLACK FISH WAS FIRST PUBLISHED IN 1969. THE STORY HAS SINCE BEEN PRINTED IN SEVERAL DIFFERENT LANGUAGES AND DISTRIBUTED ALL OVER THE WORLD.

IN 1969, THE BOOK WON A HANS CHRISTIAN ANDERSEN AWARD FOR ILLUSTRATIONS BY FARSHID MESGHALI.

OTHER AWARDS INCLUDE: IRAN'S CHILDREN'S BOOK COUNCIL AWARD (1969), BIB HONOR DIPLOMA (1970), IBBY HONOUR LIST (1974), BOLOGNA FIRST PRIZE (1970).

RESOURCES

CENTER FOR RESEARCH IN YOUNG PEOPLE'S TEXTS AND CULTURES. CRYTC. RETRIEVED FROM: HTTP://CRYTC.UWIN NIPEG.CA/RES_MAHDIAN.PHP

IRAN CHAMBER SOCIETY. (2011). IRAN CHAMBER SOCIETY. RETRIEVED FROM HTTP://WWW.IRANCHAMBER.COM/LITERA TURE/SBEHRANGI/SAMAD_BEHRANGI.PHP

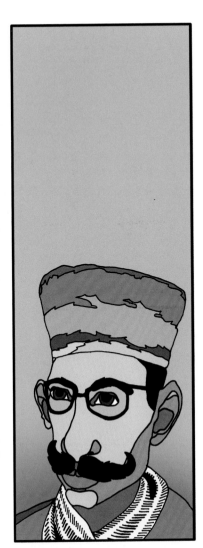

THE ART

BEHRANGI WAS ASSOCIATED WITH THE POLITICAL GROUP, THE IRANIAN PEOPLE'S FEDAI GUERRILLAS. ONE OF THE GROUP'S LEADERS WAS BIZHAN JAZANI. JAZANI ALSO HAPPENED TO BE A PHILOSOPHER AND VISUAL ARTIST. HIS PAINTINGS INSPIRED THE GRAPHIC STYLE BIZHAN KHODABANDEH CHOSE FOR THE COMIC.

THE ARTIST

BIZHAN KHODABANDEH IS A SILVER MEDAL AWARDEE FOR COMICS AND CARTOONING THROUGH THE SOCIETY OF ILLUSTRATORS. HE IS A VISUAL HO MOVES FREELY ACROSS THE PROFESSIONAL BOUNDARIES AS A DESIGNER, ILLUSTRATOR, ARTIST, AND ACTIVIST. KHODABANDEH IS PARTICULARLY FASCINATED BY HOW ART AND DESIGN CAN BE A CATALYST FOR SOCIAL CHANGE.

HE HAS RECEIVED INTERNATIONAL AND NATIONAL AWARDS FOR HIS WORK, INCLUDING PLACING IN THE ADBUSTERS' ONE FLAG COMPETITION, THE GOOD 50X70, THE GREEN PATRIOT POSTER PROJECT, POSTER FOR TOMORROW, AND RECOGNITION BY THE AMERICAN INSTITUTE FOR GRAPHIC ARTS. KHODABANDEH HAS HAD WORK FEATURED IN PUBLICATIONS SUCH AS PRINT, CREATIVITY INTERNATIONAL AND ADBUSTERS, AMONG OTHERS.

KHODABANDEH CURRENTLY TEACHES AT VIRGINIA COMMONWEALTH UNIVERSITY AND FREELANCES UNDER THE NAME MENDED ARROW.

MORE OF HIS WORK CAN BE FOUND AT: WWW.MENDEDARROW.COM

ALSO AVAILABLE FROM ROSARIUM...

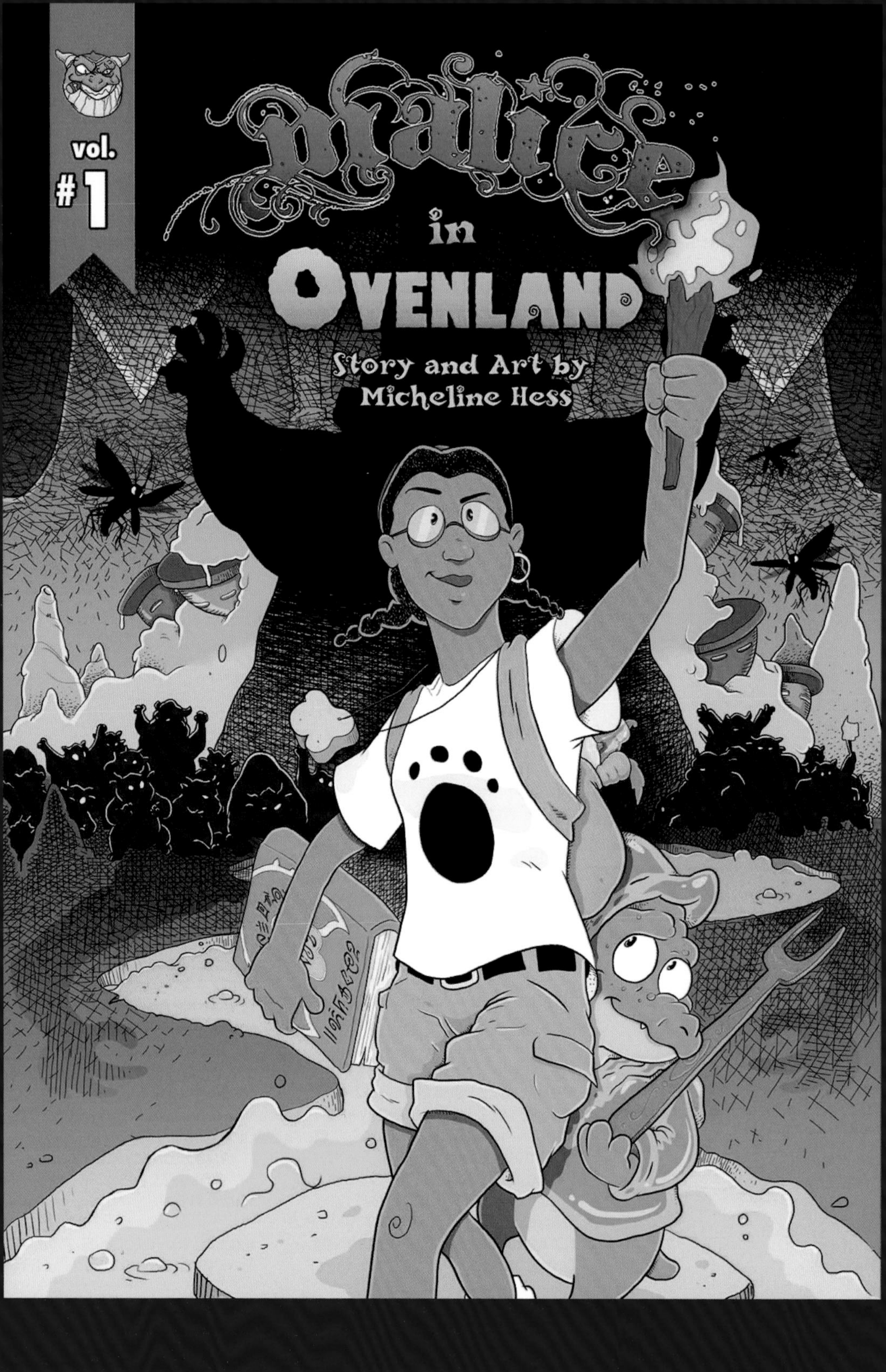
vol.
#1
Malice
in
Ovenland
Story and Art by
Micheline Hess

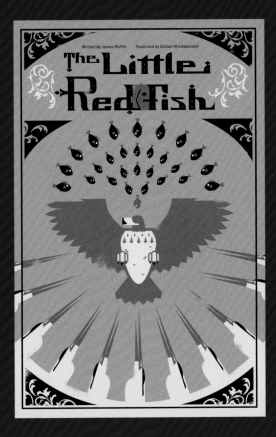

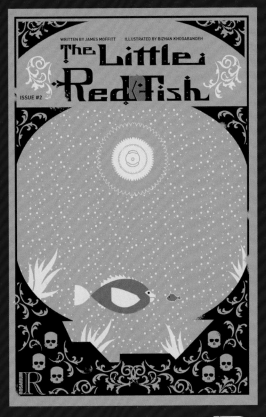

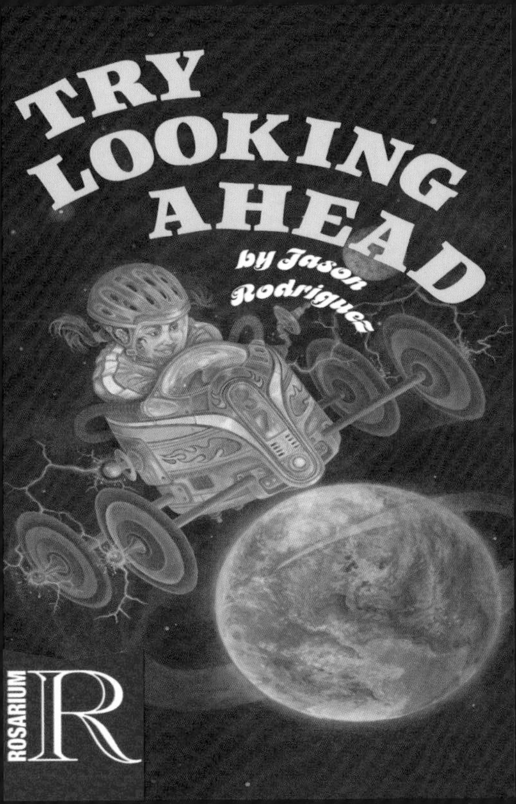
TRY LOOKING AHEAD
by Jason Rodriguez
ROSARIUM

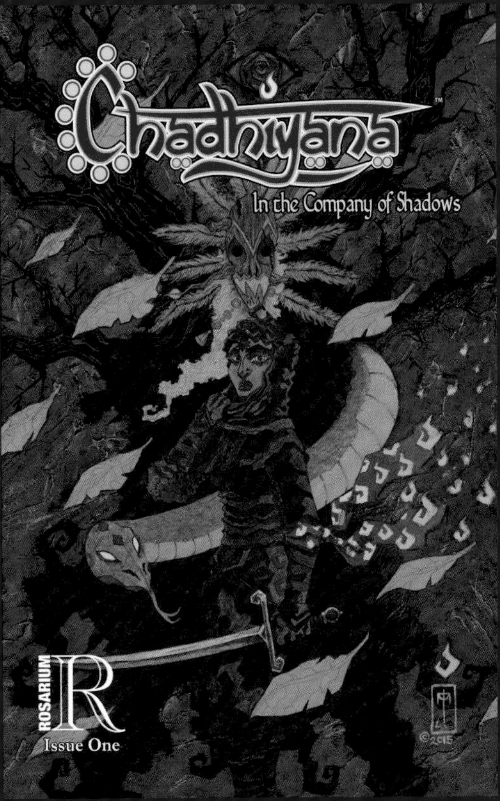
Chadhiyana
In the Company of Shadows
ROSARIUM
Issue One
©2015

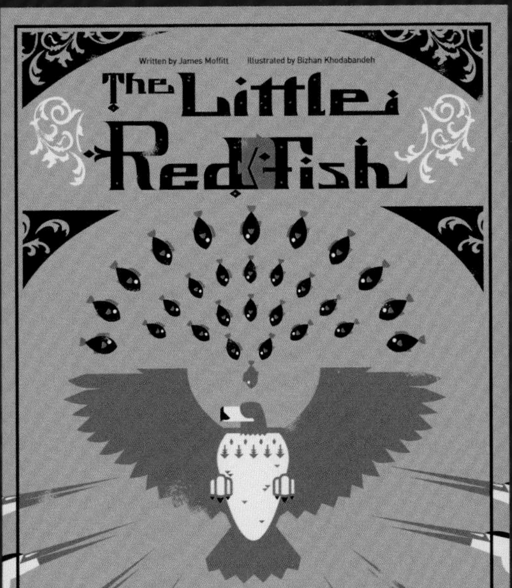
Written by James Moffitt
Illustrated by Bizhan Khodabandeh
The Little Red Fish

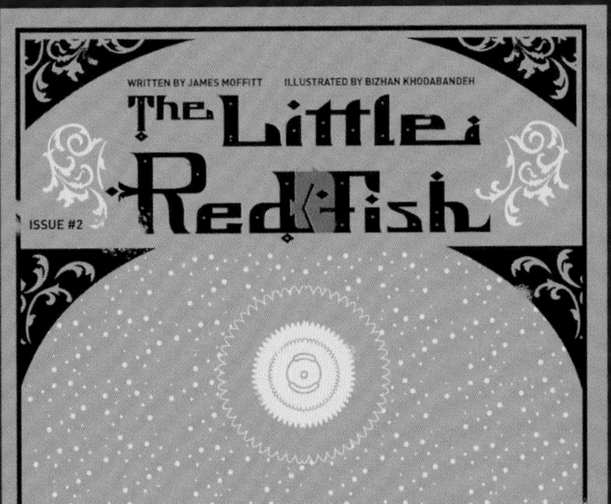
WRITTEN BY JAMES MOFFITT
ILLUSTRATED BY BIZHAN KHODABANDEH
The Little Red Fish
ISSUE #2
ROSARIUM

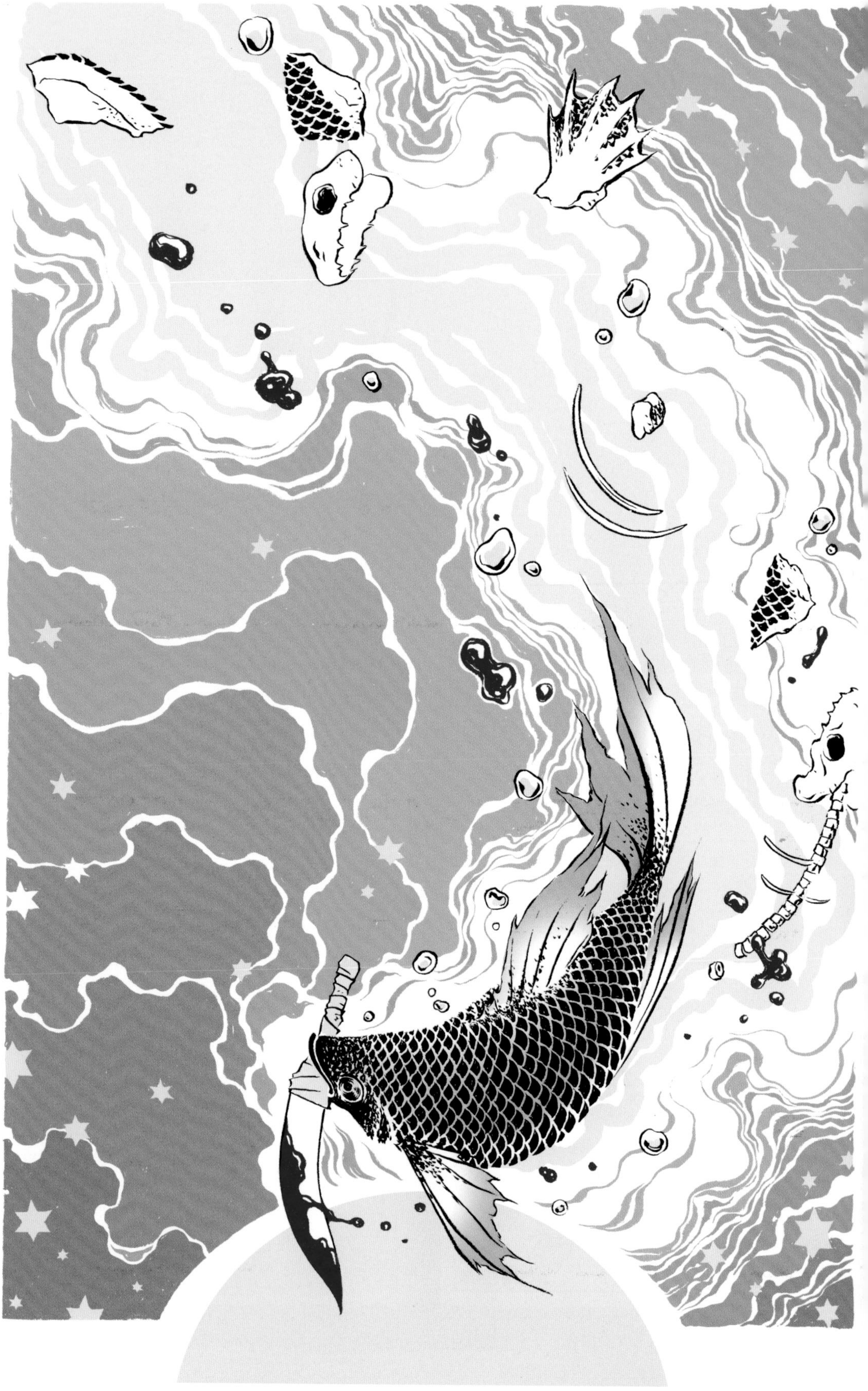

IMAGE BY MEGAN GANDY – SHATTERLANDS.COM

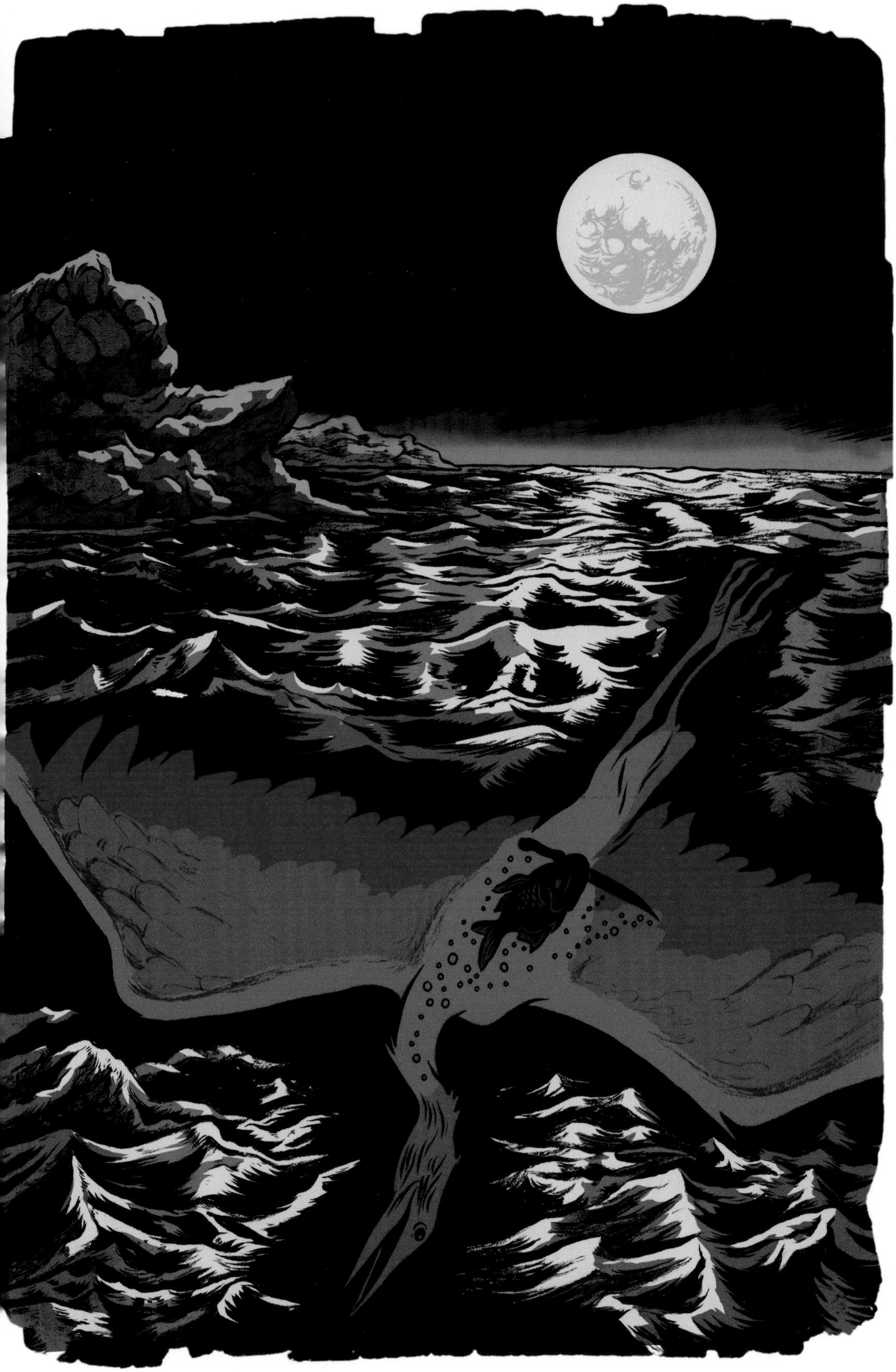

IMAGE BY MATT DEANS – TEAM-EIGHT.COM

THE LITTLE BLACK FISH

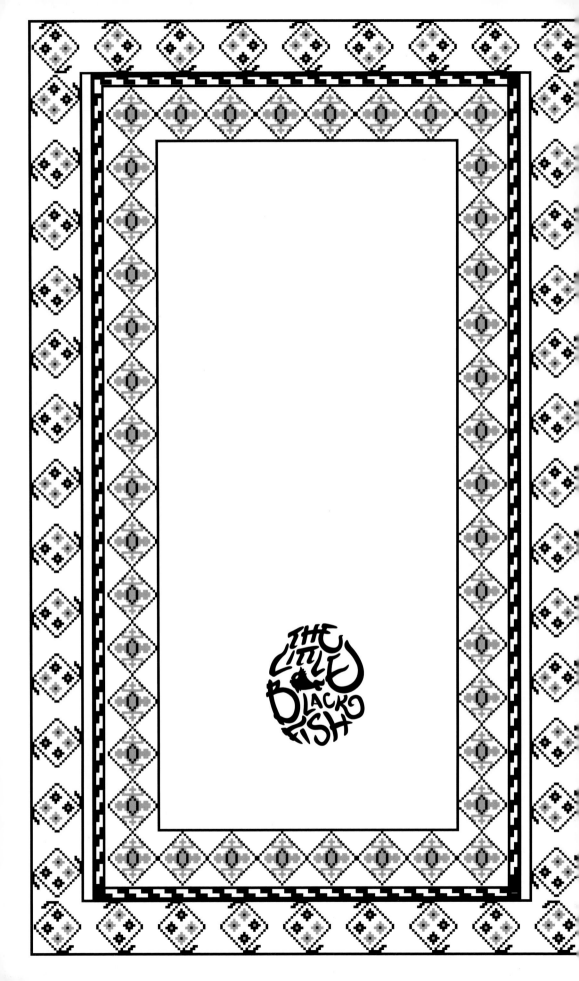

ROSARIUM

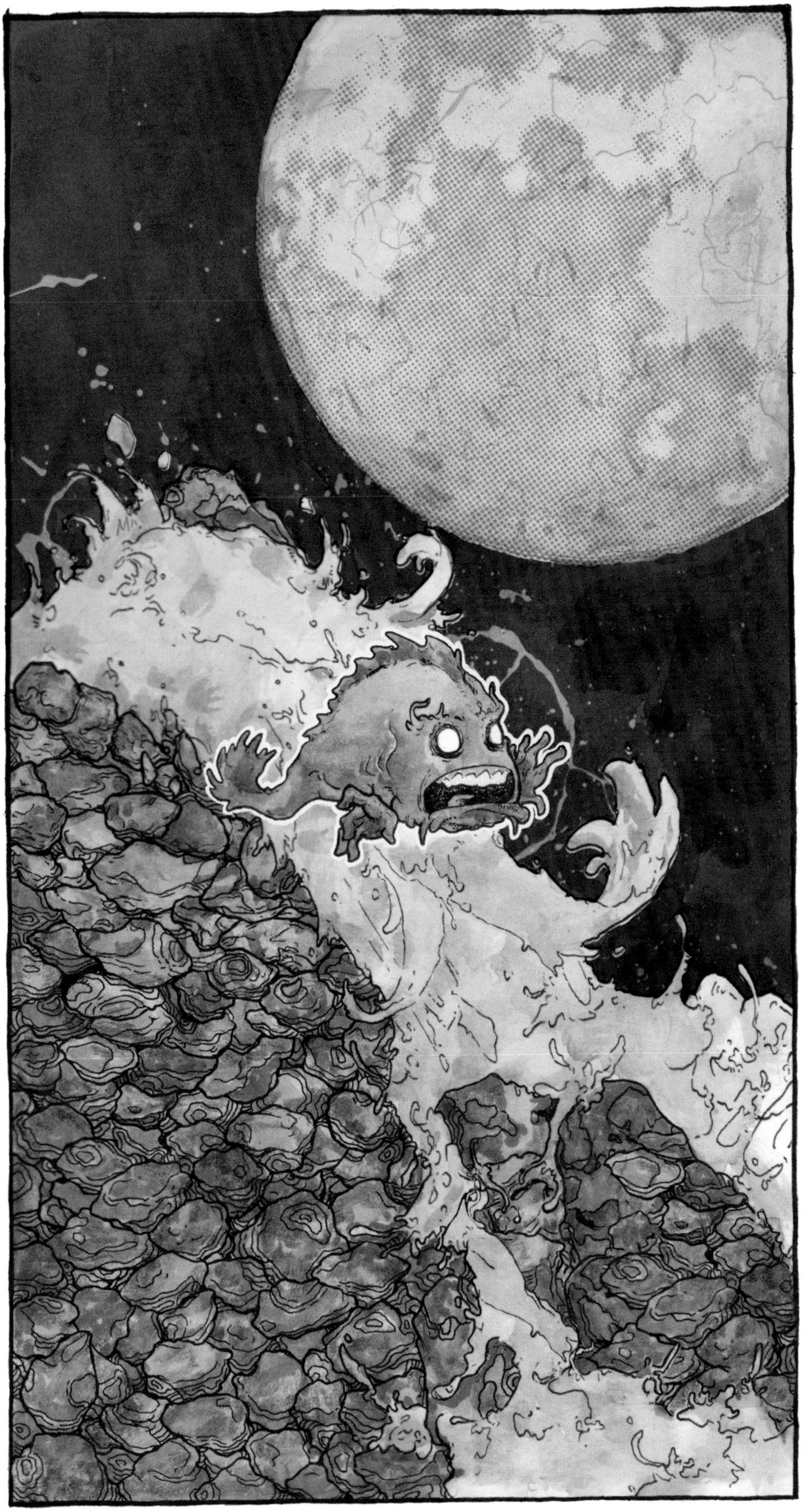

IMAGE BY RAWN GANDEY – RAWNGANDY.COM